More or Less Afraid of Nearly Everything

More or Less Afraid of Nearly Everything

Homeland Security, Borders,
and Disasters in the
Twenty-First Century

BEN ROHRBAUGH

UNIVERSITY OF MICHIGAN PRESS | ANN ARBOR

For questions or permissions, please contact um.press.perms@umich.edu

Published in the United States of America by the
University of Michigan Press
Manufactured in the United States of America
Printed on acid-free paper
First published July 2020

A CIP catalog record for this book is available from the British Library.

Library of Congress Cataloging-in-Publication Data

Names: Rohrbaugh, Ben, 1981– author.
Title: More or less afraid of nearly everything : homeland security, borders,
    and disasters in the twenty-first century / Ben Rohrbaugh.
Description: Ann Arbor : University of Michigan Press, 2020. | Includes bibliographical
    references and index. |
Identifiers: LCCN 2020013181 (print) | LCCN 2020013182 (ebook) | ISBN
    9780472074624 (hardcover) | ISBN 9780472054626 (paperback) | ISBN
    9780472127122 (ebook)
Subjects: LCSH: United States. Department of Homeland Security. | National security—
    United States. | Border security—United States. | United States—Emigration and
    immigration—Government policy.
Classification: LCC HV6432.4 .R65   2020 (print) | LCC HV6432.4 (ebook) |
    DDC 363.340973—dc23
LC record available at https://lccn.loc.gov/2020013181
LC ebook record available at https://lccn.loc.gov/2020013182

For Steph and Charlie

"Did it ever occur to you that everybody is more or less afraid of nearly everything, and that courage isn't a damned thing but a habit of not dodging things because you're afraid of them?"

—Dashiell Hammett, *The Cure*

Contents

Digital materials related to this title can be found on the Fulcrum platform via the following citable URL: https://doi.org/10.3998/mpub.11565857

Author's Note

The final version of this book was written in 2019, with the last edits to the page proofs completed in early April 2020 as my home in Austin was under a shelter-in-place order in response to the coronavirus pandemic that has already killed more than 10,000 Americans.

Rather than redraft the book to reflect the latest coronavirus developments—which would inevitably end up outdated by the time it was printed—I have kept the text largely as written and added a brief analysis of the coronavirus response in chapter 8. This approach has disadvantages: the descriptions of the problems with Ebola response seem almost quaint compared to the lurching and chaotic reaction to this disease, and I obviously would organize things differently if I were starting now.

The substance holds up, however, and the pandemic has shown just how necessary it is to rethink our security strategy. The disastrous response to coronavirus within the United States clearly supports the central arguments in this book, which are:

- Civilians are increasingly vulnerable to non-military threats.
- Our government has largely organized its security functions, however, to respond to the possibility of military action from nation-states.
- Our leaders follow strategies to keep civilians safe that are increasingly mismatched to the pandemics, terrorism, natural disasters, organized crime, cybersecurity, and other nonstate dangers to Americans and their interests.
- The organization of our government's security functions is going to change, whether as a result of deliberate decision-making or through panicked choices during disasters.
- The formation of the Department of Homeland Security was just the first, clumsy step in this process, and the difficulties that have

characterized the department's first 17 years are instructive in understanding the realignment of government that will need to occur and the difficult decisions that will need to be made.

List of Abbreviations

CBP	Customs and Border Protection
CDC	Centers for Disease Control and Prevention
CIS	Citizenship and Immigration Services
CISA	Cybersecurity and Infrastructure Security Agency
DEA	Drug Enforcement Administration
DHS	Department of Homeland Security
ESTA	Electronic System for Traveler Authorization
FAST	Free and Secure Trade
FBI	Federal Bureau of Investigation
FEMA	Federal Emergency Management Agency
FISA	Foreign Intelligence Surveillance Act
HSC	Homeland Security Council
ICE	Immigration and Customs Enforcement
ISIL	Islamic State of Iraq and the Levant
NSA	National Security Agency
NSC	National Security Council
RFID	radio frequency identification
SENTRI	Secure Electronic Network for Travelers Rapid Inspection
TIDE	Terrorist Identities Datamart Environment
TSA	Transportation Security Administration
TSDB	Terrorist Screening Database

Introduction

Ebola is a severe and awful disease, but it is actually fairly difficult to transmit: in order to become infected you need to be in contact with the blood or other bodily fluids of someone with Ebola who is demonstrating symptoms. This limits its spread; the most recent outbreak centered in West Africa killed 11,325 people over two and a half years, which is less than the tens of thousands of people killed by influenza in the United States alone each year. In 2014, after the outbreak began in Guinea and spread to Liberia and Sierra Leone, it seemed to be an international health crisis without a clear nexus to the United States. The U.S. government's response included sending a Centers for Disease Control and Prevention (CDC) team to Guinea and later 3,000 troops to Liberia to provide assistance and establish a command center, while the CDC publicly maintained the preparedness of American medical facilities for whatever happened.

And so, in mid-September 2014 when I went to work at the National Security Council (NSC) in the White House on border security policy, Ebola response was barely on my mind. It seemed clear Ebola would be dealt with by the Africa and global health experts working in other parts of the NSC, and in any case I would have my hands full enough dealing with the ongoing crisis caused by Central American migration.

The situation then changed very quickly. On September 20, a Liberian man named Thomas Eric Duncan traveled from Liberia to Dallas. On September 25 he visited the emergency room at the Texas Health Presbyterian Hospital in Dallas with fever and stomach pain, and was discharged after an examination and sent home. Three days later he was readmitted with worse symptoms and on September 30 the Ebola virus was detected in him. On that day CDC director Thomas Frieden emphasized that U.S. hospitals were well prepared to handle Ebola, saying, "One of the things we want to emphasize is virtually any hospital in the country that can do isolation, can do isolation for Ebola. We have no doubt that we will stop it in its tracks in Texas." Duncan's relatives were placed in quarantine on October 1, and he died on October 8. On October 12 a nurse who had treated Duncan at the Texas Health Presbyterian Hospital, Nina Pham, became the first person to be infected with Ebola within the United States. On the same day, the CDC stated publicly that 48 people who had interacted with Duncan before his hospitalization were at risk for Ebola. Screening passengers from Ebola-affected countries for indicators of the disease began at the five U.S. airports accepting most international flights from Liberia, Guinea, and Sierra Leone. Three days later, another nurse who had treated Duncan, Amber Joy Vinson, also tested positive for Ebola after having traveled to Cleveland and back on commercial flights.

At this point the public alarm was nearly overwhelming. House Speaker John Boehner and Texas governor Rick Perry called for blanket travel bans from the affected countries. New York, Illinois, and New Jersey imposed mandatory quarantines for anyone who had potential contact with Ebola-infected individuals. Louisiana banned researchers who had been in West Africa from the American Society of Tropical Medicine and Hygiene meeting in New Orleans. The CDC's public messaging had focused on keeping calm and the difficulty of transmission, but this seemed to have been invalidated by the new infections within the United States. The infection of the two Dallas healthcare workers in particular and the fact that over a hundred people were potentially at risk for the disease within the United States seemed to indicate that the authorities were overmatched and the situation was getting out of control.

The situation in the NSC was white knuckle. Suddenly, all of the systems and protocols that were in place needed to be stress tested to find and eliminate any additional gaps that could allow the situation to spin further out of control. Hastily convened tabletop exercises, where the participants from relevant agencies walked through how additional patients would be handled, demonstrated the urgent need to identify which facilities were really prepared to handle Ebola cases, how patients from different places would be allocated to these facilities, and how safe transportation would be organized. The Customs and Border Protection (CBP) staff who were charged with screening travelers had no particular background in dealing with Ebola and were as concerned as anyone. They needed training and protocols established that wouldn't cause Ebola scares in airports when a traveler from an affected country showed a fever. Self-monitoring for potentially exposed people was switched to direct monitoring by the CDC, and systems for tracking everyone who might have been infected and tracing all of their personal contacts needed to be quickly implemented.

My coworkers were working harder, and under more pressure, than anyone I've ever seen in my life. Everyone around got swept up in the huge amount of work that needed to be done. When you work at the NSC the most important and stressful part of the job is preparing for meetings of senior officials—the National Security Council or Homeland Security Council chaired by the president, the Principals Committees made up of cabinet secretaries and chaired by the National Security Advisor, and the Deputies Committee meetings chaired by a deputy national security advisor. In crisis situations, as this was, there would be at least one and sometimes multiple meetings at these levels each day, in addition to a constant need to brief senior leaders on status updates less formally. This meant that the staffers were working essentially continuously to gather information, compile it into meeting materials, give relevant people a brief window to comment and clear, and distribute the materials to the leaders who would be in the meetings with enough time for them to actually be read and responded to, all while trying to make sure the decisions from the previous meetings were communicated and implemented.

At this point the information that was coming in all seemed to be worse than what had come in the day before. This culminated when we found out that a worker from the Texas hospital who had handled one of Duncan's blood samples and been potentially exposed was aboard the *Carnival Magic* cruise ship off the coast of Belize. The Belizean authorities refused to allow the ship to dock to let her leave, so the worker was quarantined in her room on the ship, and the other passengers were in the sort of panic that you would expect. The situation was eventually resolved when the worker came ashore in Galveston and tested negative for Ebola, but the intervening time was excruciating for everyone involved. It also obligated NSC staffers to provide briefings with almost theatrically unwelcome titles. To come see the homeland security advisor late at night to provide a briefing on "the Ebola cruise ship situation" was to experience vivid feelings of unpopularity that most of us left behind in middle school.

The White House ended up announcing the appointment of an Ebola response coordinator (the "Ebola Czar"), bringing in Ron Klain, a senior official who had been the chief of staff to Vice Presidents Joe Biden and Al Gore. Slowly, the pressure eased and the situation began to return to normal. The two nurses from the Texas hospital both recovered, and there were no further transmissions of Ebola within the United States. The White House–led Ebola team set standards for facilities to treat Ebola and designated hospitals that could meet these to be treatment centers, expanded laboratory testing, and set clear, effective protocols for the screening and transportation of possibly sick people. It soon became clear to the public that the response was under control and effective systems were in place.

This was, in immediate terms, an example of a competent government response in a frantic situation. Institutionally, though, the experience raised serious questions about the U.S. government's preparedness and ability to respond to unexpected challenges:

- The U.S. government certainly has the resources to deal with a single infected Ebola patient, so why weren't they deployed appropriately in the Duncan case?
- How did a disease like this stretch the response capability of the U.S. government so thinly so quickly, and how much worse could the situation have been with a much more infectious disease?
- Infectious disease is hardly an unexpected threat: major SARS and H1N1 influenza scares occurred in the previous decades and the Ebola outbreak in West Africa had been going on for months. What does this mean about the preparedness for other threats that aren't as obvious?
- The initial coordinating function played by federal entities was clearly inadequate, but why hasn't an effective structure been established to actually manage medical response capabilities across different levels of government in emergencies?
- Why was the U.S. government's international response, which involved large commitments of federal resources and quickly deploying troops, so much more clear and decisive than the initial domestic response, when American civilians were directly endangered?
- If this sort of thing isn't the job of the Department of Homeland Security (DHS), why not? Why did we go through a major reorganization of government to consolidate civilian safety if the department that we created can't actually respond to all threats?
- How has the role of the NSC expanded so much that it is directly

managing disease response? Shouldn't it be focused on coordinating policy on traditional national security issues related to foreign policy and military action?

- Are future crises that fall between departments going to require the appointment of additional White House czars, or can the institutions that exist now effectively adapt?

Ebola is just one dramatic example of what seem to be increasingly difficult security problems with international and domestic implications. Whether it's an opioid crisis supplied in part by staggeringly violent transnational cartels, increasingly deadly mass shootings by extremists radicalized online, migration driven by gang violence overwhelming the government's processing capability, or outrageous breaches of individuals' most sensitive personal data by international hackers—more and more of the urgent problems facing Americans are not the ones we have organized our government to confront.

The goal of this book is to provide a framework to answer the kinds of questions raised by the Ebola response and to evaluate policy questions about homeland security and keeping civilians safe. The central argument is this: throughout the twentieth century, national security was something that the United States did not experience domestically; it defended the country by conducting military, foreign policy, and intelligence operations internationally and separated these activities from domestic law enforcement with bright legal lines. In the twenty-first century national security is no longer something that occurs in other countries. The U.S. government is only beginning to organize itself to respond to this change, and the establishment of the Department of Homeland Security is just the first step in an organizational and strategic realignment that will be a long, difficult, and mistake-filled process.

Civilians, their interests, and critical institutions have become vulnerable on a scale that in the past could only have been threatened by overt action by hostile nation-states. This change has been caused by interconnected societal and technological shifts. This is not a normal situation for Americans. Throughout the twentieth century the prospect of a direct attack on American civilians existed mainly in the context of a catastrophic world war, but the wars that did occur all happened elsewhere. Only in recent decades have Americans experienced mass casualty attacks on civilians in American cities, threats to essential civilian infrastructure like utilities or communications systems, foreign states using indirect proxies to conduct significant interference in core democratic processes, major movements of displaced and vulnerable populations directly to U.S. territory, the massive theft of extremely sensitive personal and financial information from businesses or government, increasingly devastating natural disasters, and the possibility of weapons of mass destruction delivered by actors who are not deterred by the threat of massive retaliation. What happened on 9/11 showed how poorly prepared the U.S. government was to respond to a novel attack by trained terrorist operatives exploiting vulnerabilities created by the expansion of air travel. Vulnerabilities on a similar scale are developing or already exist in other areas, such as digital networks, biological laboratories, and even less obvious places. The U.S. government is having just as much trouble responding to these as it did to terrorist travel before the disastrous forcing function of 9/11 created huge pressure for change.

These shifts have profound strategic implications for American security, and our institutions are just beginning the processes of adapting. The government made dramatic changes to its counterterrorism and border control functions after the 9/11 attacks, but the rest of the American security enterprise and our strategic and legal frameworks are still largely organized to address direct threats from nation-states. The American government is still fundamentally resourced and structured to use military force and intelligence operations internationally and to conduct law enforcement operations domestically. The federal role in disaster response and emergency medical response is largely a coordinating function.

Reorientations of government are never smooth or pleasant for the people and institutions involved. Government agencies, like all bureaucracies, have certain institutional worldviews and recruit and train people to achieve within them. They are led, largely, by officials who have spent their careers ascending the organization's hierarchy, and have enormous incentives to want to continue succeeding within that organization on familiar terms. One of the most difficult things for a government entity to do is to change a strategy that has previously been successful, especially if it is led by people who have devoted their careers to that strategy. Major shifts in government are also made difficult because they create opportunities for significant overreach and unexpected abuses of power for which effective checks have not yet been established. This is because new strategies stretch legal authorities and are hard for oversight regimes to keep up with, and quickly shifting resources always creates new opportunities for fraud, waste, and abuse.

The central challenge for citizens and policymakers is to manage this process as well as is possible, and to directly and honestly confront the very difficult questions that will inevitably be presented. Refocusing on domestic national security threats to civilians and institutions while maintaining effective government and vital constitutional protections will require vigilance, particularly in terms of executive branch leadership, congressional and public oversight, appropriate legislative changes, and effective judicial review of the government as it responds to new threats. Executive branch leaders will have to push departments to do things they do not want to do that conflict with strategies that have previously been successful. Overseers will need to recognize that an agency that is taking on a new role and grappling with new or expanded challenges will always make significant mistakes, and overseers will have to go beyond identifying and punishing incompetence to managing a process of change. Legislators will need to reallocate resources significantly, particularly through massive increases in resources devoted to protecting civilians domestically—the kinds of expenditures that we have previously only associated with international military operations. They will also need to make limited and appropriate changes to the legal regime, especially as the traditional lines between domestic and international security further blur, to prevent officials from feeling obligated or empowered to take illegal actions in the name of public safety. Judicial review will need to similarly manage this shift rather than react against changes—a judge who expansively rejects the government's ability to establish watch lists as unconstitutional will make it more likely that executive branch officials will ignore constitutional restraints entirely in response to a crisis.

American political leaders have an obligation to forthrightly address this process and communicate honestly with the public, rather than exploit the inevitable tensions caused by change for political gain. They have largely ignored this responsibility, and Americans are very poorly served by the political discussion of homeland security issues. If public figures and policymakers use outdated foreign policy and military frameworks to evaluate homeland security issues, they will inevitably make mistakes with significant consequences. Failing to adapt our strategic, organizational, and legal systems to the new challenges does not mean that change will be avoided or delayed; it means that it will occur in the aftermath of a disaster, guaranteeing frantic decision-making and making unsustainable systems or significant overreach much more likely. In 2019 we are seeing this most dramatically in the area of migration, where a government frustrated by huge numbers of asylum seekers at the Southwest border and unable to respond effectively within existing laws and policies is responding with increasingly extreme and extralegal measures.

It will always be more comfortable to respond to threats with familiar approaches to security—this is exemplified by the lead up to and execution of the Iraq War. In response to a new and uncertain threat, the George W. Bush administration, with nearly unanimous support from major national security, political, and media figures, responded to an attack from a decentralized and nonstate twenty-first-century terrorist group by invading an unrelated hostile nation-state. This was at the time much more natural for everyone involved than dealing with complex questions about wiretapping authority or watch lists: the White House knew how to make a public case for an invasion, the Defense Department knew how to destroy a foreign military, the State Department knew how to engage international institutions and foreign counterparts in this context, Congress knew how to provide funding and oversight of military operations, and journalists knew how to cover wars. The aftermath also shows, however, how applying a twentieth-century strategy of invading nation-states as a means of stopping twenty-first-century terrorism is strategically disastrous.

I've spent the last decade immersed in homeland security as a senior advisor at DHS, as a counselor to four commissioners of Customs and Border Protection, coordinating border security policy for the NSC in the White House, and in the private sector as a consultant and the founder of a company developing autonomous systems for cargo security, and have struggled to understand a strategic approach to modern security. When I began working at DHS, the responses to strategic questions mostly began with a phrase like "In the wake of 9/11 . . ." and then described the new programs that had been put in place. This was reasonable enough: "9/11 can never happen again" is a good justification for the changes we have made to our aviation security or traveler vetting enterprise. It has much less explanatory power, however, for responding to twenty-first-century refugee and asylum seekers, or the DHS approach to cybersecurity. The framework presented in this book has been extremely useful to me to evaluate and understand homeland security issues, and I hope that this book will help interested non-experts better engage these questions. Homeland security can often be an extremely technical subject, but there are major questions that will need to be decided in the coming years and these decisions should not be left entirely up to specialists or only to practitioners within DHS. Any department that exercises authorities over every item and person that moves into the United States and spends many tens of billion dollars a year is of interest to every citizen, and there should be broad participation in debates about its future.

This book is organized to provide a conceptual understanding of the way security is changing and a practical understanding of how the government has changed to this point, with a deep dive on the evolving response to border management and migration that provides an extended case study with implications for other areas of homeland security.

The first two chapters explain how civilians have become more vulnerable, the societal and technological shifts that have brought national security threats directly to the United States, and the implications of these shifts on how security must be approached.

The third chapter shows how government has changed to this point and what has gone well and what hasn't, with a particular emphasis on the important decisions that were addressed when DHS was created and the other urgent questions that remain unresolved.

Chapter 4 provides detailed background on DHS as it exists and operates today. It also provides recommendations on how to think about policy decisions in a homeland security context, which need a different kind of framework than foreign policy and national security decisions.

Chapters 5, 6, and 7 provide a deep dive into the areas of borders and migration, which have been the focus of much of the changes that have been instituted to this point. The ambition to make this book brief and accessible directly conflicted with any possibility of comprehensiveness, so these three chapters focus on the area that has been most thoroughly consolidated within DHS and ongoing political flashpoints. This provides practical examples of the concepts explained in the first chapter and will provide lessons and insights that can be applied to other policy areas. Chapter 5 demonstrates how border management developed into the twentieth-century approach, chapter 6 shows how that is now being supplanted by an approach based on risk segmentation and targeting, and chapter 7 addresses the particular challenges of rapidly changing migration flows.

Chapter 8 identifies three particularly challenging areas that the government has not yet successfully organized itself to respond to, and discusses the kinds of policy and regulatory changes that will likely be necessary:

- Cybersecurity;
- Transnational organized crime; and
- Emergency medical response.

The very term "homeland security" can be a source of dispute or confusion, with some seeing it as ominous or representing the kind of post-9/11 chauvinism that led the first major counterterrorism legislation to be called Uniting and Strengthening America by Providing Appropriate Tools Required to Intercept and Obstruct Terrorism (USA-PATRIOT). It is necessary, however, to have a way to describe security issues that fall outside of the traditional domestic law enforcement and international military and intelligence spheres. Other terms would have worked as well or better: the department could have just as reasonably been called "Civil Defense," "Domestic Preparedness," or "Public Safety" (as is its Canadian equivalent). Homeland security is the term we've been left with, and in this book I use it to describe the work of the government to protect civilians and their interests from nonmilitary threats.

Lastly, after spending eight years working within DHS, I have seen firsthand how the overuse of acronyms frequently manages to take written materials that were already fairly confusing and make them completely impenetrable. This is often coupled with an almost charming lack of awareness of double meanings—I used to regularly receive invitations to an SOB working group (State Of the Border) and get urgent demands from the department's executive secretary for status updates on the secretary's BMs (they meant Briefing Memos). As such, this work avoids acronyms as much as is reasonably feasible, although I will use the common abbreviations of the names of federal departments (e.g., State, Defense, Treasury). I also tried and failed to avoid using the common acronyms for the DHS components and other major law enforcement agencies (TSA, ICE, CBP, DEA, FBI, and so forth); writing them out each time was just intolerably clunky. DHS refers to the Department of Homeland Security, "homeland security" in lower case refers to the concept, and the term "homeland security enterprise" is used to describe all of the elements of the U.S. government involved in homeland security work, both within and outside of the department.

1 | National Security Comes Home

This chapter expands the book's central argument, which is that national security is no longer something that happens in other countries and that the creation of DHS and the counterterrorism enterprise are just the beginning of the process of adaptation.

Throughout the twentieth century the principal existential threats to American civilians and the constitutional order of the government were based in hostile foreign nation-states. The preponderant military and unique geographical situation of the United States, however, meant that these threats were confronted internationally. This was an extremely unusual experience of the twentieth century; civilians of most other countries in the world experienced traumatic conflict directly within their own territory. The American domestic preparedness efforts of the twentieth century, such as the governor's councils established during World War I and the civil defense initiatives under President Franklin Roosevelt, were all focused on the threat of a foreign invasion, and were in each case disbanded after the end of the war.[1] The Cold War threat of a nuclear attack quickly became so devastating that it exceeded any possible civil response capability, and only the deterrence of a massive guaranteed response could provide effective protection.

The situation has changed. The overwhelming capabilities of the American military and nuclear response continue to deter any direct military threats. Nonstate actors and quasi-state proxy organizations, however, are becoming much more dangerous for civilians. There are two major reasons for this change. The first is technological advances that have created major new vulnerabilities and correspondingly empowered smaller organizations to exploit them. These vulnerabilities also amplify the impacts of natural disasters, which are escalating because of climate change.

The second reason is that nonstate groups are fundamentally changing. This is driven by a societal change in developed countries where the state increasingly provides greater individual freedom and economic opportunity and is much less focused on guarantees of well-being for a cohesive citizenry. The shift from the nation-states that dominated the twentieth century, which attempted to maximize the overall welfare of citizens, to market-states, which prioritize maximizing individual opportunity, is reflected in the methods and aims of terrorist and criminal groups that challenge the prevailing society. Twenty-first-century terrorist and criminal organizations are quite different from their twentieth-century counterparts and are not deterred by the prospect of a military response, which is most alarming in the prospect of proliferating weapons of mass destruction. State-backed challenges as well will likely be indirect and use proxies and other asymmetric methods that will make military responses uncertain and awkwardly matched.

The result of these shifts is that civilians and the institutions upon which they rely are now endangered at a scale that has previously only been associated with military attacks by a nation-state. This is an enormous change. The legitimacy of the U.S. government depends upon its guarantees of a certain level of safety, but to continue to provide that level of safety it will have to realign and reorganize its security functions. The creation of DHS and the counterterrorism enterprise are the first steps in the shift toward vastly expanded prevention and response capabilities directed at nonstate actors and the specific threats they pose.

The emerging threats are widely recognized, but effectively adapting to them is extremely difficult. There are regular news stories about the vulnerabilities of digital networks that are increasingly critical to modern life, escalating natural disasters driven by climate change, and most alarmingly the continued proliferation of weapons of mass destruction. These are not marginal threats. First, many more people could be directly harmed than has occurred in the past. The 9/11 attacks killed 2,977 people,[2] and Hurricane Katrina killed 1,833.[3]* Credible estimates of the fatalities from a terrorist attack using biological or nuclear weapons against a major city range from tens of thousands to millions.[4] This level of devastation would be obviously intolerable. Second, failures to keep citizens safe and essential institutions functional endanger the existing constitutional order. A

---

* As of April 7, 2020, when this book was finalized, the coronavirus pandemic had already killed more than 10,000 people in America and leaders were openly talking about the possibility of hundreds of thousands of deaths. The spread of the virus has shown how horrifyingly vulnerable civilians have become to nonstate threats.

world in which a terrorist nuclear attack or biological weapon had killed tens of thousands of people or more in American cities would be unrecognizably different from our own: officials without adequate preparation and faced with threats they don't understand can be expected to overreach drastically. This is a particularly urgent concern during the administration of President Donald Trump, when an attack would clearly result in massively repressive responses unconstrained by constitutional limitations.

In this analysis 9/11 was not a one-off event but an alarming demonstration of the threats that will continue to grow in the twenty-first century. The good news is that after 9/11 we adapted effectively to traveler vetting and disrupting terrorist organizations, which has been demonstrated by the destruction of al Qaeda's leadership and the prevention of a similar attack since. The bad news is that it took the forcing function of 9/11 to make this happen and that we will have to undergo comparable processes for other areas including cybersecurity, health security, mass migration, and climate-driven natural disasters.

Organizing military, intelligence, and foreign policy efforts to effectively respond to twentieth-century state-based threats was a long and difficult process. The Department of Defense was created by combining the Departments of War, the Army, the Navy, and the newly separate Air Force through the National Security Act of 1947, which also established the Central Intelligence Agency, the National Security Council, and the Joint Chiefs of Staff. It took Defense decades to overcome the coordination problems caused by this merger and even then it was a work in progress. A series of major disasters caused in part by rivalries and lack of communication between the different services, including the Vietnam War and the Iranian hostage rescue mission in 1980, led to a full-scale reorganization through the Goldwater-Nichols Act of 1986. Major abuses of law enforcement and intelligence authorities, particularly the domestic spying on citizens that was revealed by the Church Committee in 1975, led to bright lines being drawn between the activities that were acceptable internationally and domestically and an expanded legal and oversight structure.

Chronologically, we are about as far through the current shift as the United States was in 1963 during the last one. Continuing this transition will be extremely difficult and messy, as the American government's security functions and corresponding oversight have been extremely effective at the projects for which they were organized: confronting international fascism and communism while providing effective law enforcement and avoiding unacceptable levels of domestic repression. Unfortunately, the public political discussion about these issues has little to do with the most urgent questions we face and is often actively harmful.

This chapter will now provide a detailed explanation of the changes that are occurring, the implications for the national security enterprise, and the steps that need to be taken to manage this process as smoothly as possible while avoiding overreach and maintaining accountability.

Technological Advances Have Made Civilians More Vulnerable and Made Systems Less Resilient

Technological changes have enabled people, money, and information to move much more quickly, reorganized the world economy through distributed production networks, and led to unprecedented concentrations of people in urban areas. These changes have created and expanded corresponding vulnerabilities.

People move further and faster for less. The availability of mass air travel and the widespread adoption of automobiles has meant that travelers move around the world and cross international borders much more quickly and less predictably than has ever been possible in the past. Air travel has grown consistently since the Second World War, with international air travel doubling every five years between 1950 and 2000.[5] In 2016 there were over 3.8 billion air travelers, according to the International Air Travel Association.[6]

People also live much closer together in urban areas. The early twenty-first century is the first time more than half of the world's population lives in cities, and the proportion is far higher in developed countries. In the United States, as of 2010, 80.7 percent of the population lived in cities.[7] Much of the new building has been done in areas prone to fires, floods, and earthquakes, with little thought to the implications of a changing climate.[8] These concentrations of people and constant physical movements of people between cities around the world have created remarkable economic opportunities, but also mean that the effects of natural disasters, pandemic diseases, and terrorist attacks are all amplified.

As demonstrated by the example of Ebola in the introduction, diseases can now spread extremely quickly. The threat of pandemic disease is continuously increasing, and outbreaks will cause enormous panic and disruption. There have been pandemics on a much larger scale in the past than have occurred recently, one of the most notable being the strain of influenza that killed between 20 and 40 million people around the world in 1918–19.[9] A comparably deadly virus today would surely spread much more quickly due to denser urban populations and expanded travel networks.

The remarkable medical advances that protected civilians from disease during the last century are paradoxically creating new vulnerabilities. Diseases are evolving as they are exposed to antibiotics, making them more deadly and complicating other medical procedures. Effective antibiotics are necessary to treat diseases but are also essential for a broad range of medical procedures including surgery and chemotherapy. The World Health Organization in January 2018 identified antimicrobial resistance as "an increasingly serious threat to global public health that requires action across all government sectors and society," and identified tuberculosis, malaria, influenza, and HIV as diseases that have been becoming more drug-resistant.[10]

The spread of internet connectivity has led to astonishing changes in the availability of information. As of 2017 over half of the world's population is estimated to have internet access for the first time.[11] This drives a relentless increase in the amount of specialized information that is available to everyone, with particularly significant results for homeland security. Terrorist groups have been remarkably adept at exploiting this technology. Social media provides an instant network to radicalizing individuals, and it is easier than ever before to gain detailed instructions on homemade weapons. More significantly, detailed technical information about weapons of mass destruction is now much more broadly available than it has ever been.

The cost of communication has moved very quickly toward zero. In the last few decades we have seen a progression from free emails to free calls over the internet to essentially unlimited free communication. Now, ubiquitous mobile phones and encrypted communications applications have enabled individual citizens to communicate immediately with networks of people around the world.

The spread of internet-connected devices has led to the introduction of code into a vastly increased number of products and appliances. The proliferation of devices connected to the internet has introduced software into nearly all of the new appliances and vehicles that Americans operate, as well as places that are generally unexpected (such as 911 systems).[12] Companies are adding software focused on features and functions largely without considering the resilience of the system—functions are now being performed by software that does not meet the standards of durability and redundancy that an engineered process would have required. The risks of this are vividly demonstrated in James Somers's article "The Coming Software Apocalypse":[13]

> It's been said that software is "eating the world." More and more, critical systems that were once controlled mechanically, or by people, are coming to depend on code. This was perhaps never clearer than in the summer of 2015, when on a single day, United Airlines grounded its fleet because of a problem with its departure-management system; trading was suspended on the New York Stock Exchange after an upgrade; the front page of *The Wall Street Journal's* website crashed; and Seattle's 911 system went down again, this time because a different router failed. The simultaneous failure of so many software systems smelled at first of a coordinated cyber-attack. Almost more frightening was the realization, late in the day, that it was just a coincidence.

The alarming anecdotes about new vulnerabilities seem endless. In 2015 Chrysler recalled 1.4 million vehicles after hackers demonstrated they could access a Jeep Cherokee's digital systems remotely and control the vehicle, overriding the driver. In 2017 a DHS-sponsored team of hackers claimed to have gained remote access to the controls of a Boeing 757.[14]

The increased worldwide flows of people and information have been accompanied by a huge increase in international financial flows. The establishment in 1973 of the Society for Worldwide Interbank Financial Transfers (SWIFT) established common standards for financial transactions and data for the first time, meaning that international commerce no longer depended on banks having multiple foreign branches or agreements with specific foreign counterpart banks. As a result of this, cross-border flows of goods, services, and finance grew from $3 trillion in 1980 to $36 trillion in 2012.[15] Money can now be moved, and stolen, at a previously unimaginable speed and scale.

The spread of containerization for cargo and international supply chains, combined with manufacturing systems that allow efficient manufacturing processes to be distributed across different locations, has also driven extraordinary economic changes. Containerization didn't make transporting goods faster, it made loading and unloading them faster, with the result that the overall process became enormously cheaper. Up until the 1950s and the development of standardized containers it was incredibly labor intensive to load and unload ships: in 1951 over 410,000 people in New York City had jobs directly tied to goods arriving by port, out of a total employed population of 3,008,364.[16] Now, essentially all of those jobs have disappeared, and 90 percent of the goods that the developed world consumes arrive by ship.[17]

Containerization has been closely linked with the rise of what are commonly called "just in time" manufacturing systems, which identify the costs of carrying inventory and prevent components from being manufactured until they were actually needed. This innovation, combined with containerization, means that every step of a manufacturing process can be done in the most cost-effective location. Prior to this, manufacturing could be done most efficiently on an assembly line in a central location and trade flows primarily consisted of raw materials moving from undeveloped countries to developed countries, and then finished goods moving from developed countries around the world. Now, many industrial processes have been spread out to different locations with lower production costs, resulting in much more interconnected supply chains.[18] This has provided the world with inexpensive goods, but also has provided extensive opportunities for organized crime and other bad actors to infiltrate the complex flows of legal goods.

These changes have three major security implications:

1. Rapid changes introduce unexpected vulnerabilities that governments are slow to address.
2. American civilians and corporations now have interests around the world that can be affected by international entities.
3. The changes have made systems more interdependent and less resilient.

Rapid technological changes remove resilience and introduce new and unexpected vulnerabilities. This was dramatically shown by the 9/11 hijackers' exploitation of the insecurities of commercial air travel to conduct a mass casualty terror attack. This has happened before in other contexts. In the 1930s the broad availability of automobiles caused an interstate crime wave involving multiple heavily armed gangs conducting violent bank robberies, including the Dillinger gang, Bonnie Parker and

Clyde Barrow, George "Machine Gun Kelly" Barnes, the Barker gang, and others. This new type of criminal was so dangerous and overwhelming for existing police departments that they forced the relationship between federal, state, and local law enforcement to fundamentally change and caused the establishment of the Federal Bureau of Investigation (FBI) as a national police force.[19]

When technological innovations have economic benefits the initial government response is to support and further enable the changes. It is only after the vulnerabilities have been demonstrated that they are addressed. This is exemplified by the U.S. government's reaction to the expansion of air travel. As passenger travel grew and grew the U.S. government removed many of the traveler security measures that had previously existed, reducing physical inspections and adding a customs "green lane" for people with nothing to declare. The requirement that travelers obtain visas was eliminated for travelers from the United Kingdom and Japan in 1988 and by 2001 it had been expanded to the point that half of all travelers were from countries from which the United States no longer required visas.[20] This meant that the United States had essentially no advance information about who it was admitting. This was done despite the fact that none of the countries in the visa waiver program shared criminal information with the U.S. government.[21]

Another result of this is that American citizens and corporations have interests around the world and that American interests are accessible to people located outside of American territory in new ways. These vulnerabilities are well documented, and officials and other public figures have talked about the possibility of an attack on these systems in the form of a "Cyber 9/11" so frequently that it has practically become a cliché: Defense Secretary Leon Panetta warned that the United States was in a "pre-9/11 moment" in terms of cybersecurity in 2012;[22] in 2017 the Homeland Security Advisory Council warned that the United States was not prepared for a "Cyber 9/11";[23] and the Atlantic Council think tank formed a Cyber 9/12 Student Challenge in 2017[24] to examine what would need to be done the day after an attack. The concerns are real. It is not difficult to think of entities that, if hacked by malicious actors, could cause major damage and mass panic: the pharmaceutical plants where medicines are mixed, the air traffic control system, energy infrastructure in major cities, dams, essential food supplies—the list can go on and on. In one particularly scary demonstration of how this could look in the future, in 2016 the Justice Department revealed that hackers associated with the Iranian government had infiltrated the controls of a dam in upstate New York, and were unable to operate the controls only because they had been manually disconnected for maintenance.[25] As will be discussed in detail later, however, the U.S. government has not been effective in organizing itself to respond to these threats.

Societal Shifts Have Made Civilians More Vulnerable

These technological advances have been intertwined with a fundamental change to the organizing purpose of government—which has essential implications for American security strategy. Philip Bobbitt, in the books *The Shield of Achilles* and *Terror and Consent*, described the transition from the nation-states that provided the dominant constitutional order of the twentieth century to the concept of twenty-first-century market-states, and the different claims they use as the basis of their legitimacy.

Bobbitt describes how nation-states based their sovereignty on their ability to defend their territorial borders and to maintain supreme control over law within those borders. Challenges to that sole sovereignty within a state's borders are therefore challenges to nation-states themselves. Following the end of the Cold War this control is increasingly being challenged by international standards of human rights, proliferating weapons of mass destruction that leave states unable to guarantee their safety, nonstate threats moving quickly across national borders, an international economic structure largely beyond state control, and an international communications network that treats borders as irrelevant. This is then contrasted with the emerging market-state that structures itself in response to these changes:

> Like the nation-state, the market-state assesses its economic success or failure by its society's ability to secure more and better goods and services, but in contrast to the nation-state it does not see the State as more than a minimal provider or redistributor. Whereas the nation-state justified itself as an instrument to serve the welfare of the people (the nation), the market-state exists to maximize the opportunities enjoyed by all members of society.[26]

The United States is in the process of transitioning from a nation-state to a market-state, but the process is not complete. The Trump administration epitomizes the backlash against this shift and an attempt to revert to the systems and strategies of twentieth-century American nationalism, with aggressively nation-state-based "America First" strategies, nostalgic emphasis on America's former greatness, and support almost solely from ethnic white voters. The subsequent chapters will explain how unlikely these strategies are to be successful in the twenty-first century.

This framework is extremely powerful in understanding the changing forms of terrorism, organized crime, migration, pandemic disease, cybersecurity, and other challenges that confront American homeland security officials. For the purposes of this book, these are the most significant implications:

1. Market-state terrorists and organized crime will evolve to mirror the constitutional order in which they operate in disturbing ways—most significantly by being much more lethal for civilians than their counterparts were in the twentieth century;
2. Challenges from hostile states will be conducted indirectly and take advantage of the attributes of market-states to conduct attacks that fall into categories we currently define as homeland security, such as using proxies to exploit weaknesses in digital networks, while seeking weapons of mass destruction to deter attack from more powerful counterparts; and
3. Disasters around the world, whether caused by humans or not, will affect the United States and other developed countries much more directly than they have in the past, and our existing systems of managing migration and asylum seekers will be increasingly mismatched and indefensible.

Market-State Terrorism Seeks Spectacular Devastation

The goals and activities of market-state terrorists will be different from their twentieth-century predecessors, and they will be much more interested in spectacular attacks and obtaining weapons of mass destruction. As Bobbitt says of the transition from nation-states to market-states in *Terror and Consent*: "This transition will change the nature of terrorism because terrorism . . . is an incident of the underlying constitutional order. Different constitutional orders spawn different terrorisms."[27]

Nation-state terrorists sought to challenge the ability of the prevailing state to guarantee the welfare of the nation and to legitimate their own claims for recognition within the world of nation-states, always self-described as a liberation movement. This meant using violence against civilians as a tactic but often targeted at a specific ethnic group and within the limitations imposed by their efforts to obtain international sympathy for their cause. The first examples of market-state terrorist groups, al Qaeda and the Islamic State of Iraq and the Levant (ISIL), recognize no such limitations on their actions—maximum violence against civilians is an end in itself.

Twenty-first-century terrorist groups will increasingly challenge the legitimacy of the state by attempting to destroy its ability to provide opportunities through spectacular attacks. These are the essential characteristics of market-state terrorism:[28]

1. It is more lethal to civilians and is not responsive to concerns about backlash against its actions;
2. It is better financed than nation-state counterparts were and takes advantage of international financial networks to fund operations from a broader range of sources and to hide the movement of funds;
3. Organizations are decentralized and use a franchise model to outsource activities broadly to local chapters, providing training and resources rather than maintaining hierarchical control;
4. Market-state terrorists capitalize on technology to communicate and plan, obtain information about weapons, radicalize new recruits, and amplify the public messaging around their activities;
5. It is interested in obtaining weapons of mass destruction and *would not hesitate to use them*, unlike nation-state terrorists who wished to avoid the massive international response this would provoke;
6. It actively attempts to generate videos of increasingly horrific scenes to seize public attention and cause terror;
7. Its ultimate targets are the leading market-states to date, primarily the United States and the European Union; and
8. Terrorism is no longer a tactic to obtain control of a nation-state, but instead an end in itself, to negate a new constitutional order they cannot tolerate.

The clearest demonstration of the change is in the attitude of these groups toward weapons of mass destruction. Nationalist terror groups in the twentieth century wanted to take over the government of their state, and using weapons of mass destruction wouldn't make sense in that context. As an example of the shift, in 1992, 1993, and 1996, the nation-state terrorist group the Irish Republican Army detonated vehicle bombs in key London financial centers, and in each instance they called in a warning to authorities about an hour before the bomb went off. There were still fatalities and injuries, largely to first responders who were evacuating the areas, but far fewer than there would have been if there had been no warning of the bombings.[29] It is impossible to imagine a group like ISIL calling in an advance warning for an attack of this kind, because it would defeat the purpose of their actions. In 1998 Osama bin Laden issued a public proclamation announcing his intention to obtain and use nuclear weapons against civilians.[30]

It is essential to recognize that future market-state terrorist groups may not resemble the ones we have seen to date. Market-state terrorists may be ideologically fairly flexible, as is shown clearly by the evolution in Iraq of members of Saddam Hussein's Fedayeen paramilitary force into key members of Abu Musab al-Zarqawi's al Qaeda affiliate during the Iraqi insurgency and subsequently into the operational leaders of ISIL.[31] The most important thing is how developed these groups are and the resources to which they have access: money, areas in which to operate without state harassment, recruits with military training, the ability to exploit international travel networks, and weapons. Much of the reason that al Qaeda has been so incredibly deadly is that it was able to develop all of the capabilities identified above: it had enormous financial resources through the inherited fortune of Osama bin Laden, it had areas in Sudan and Afghanistan from which to plan operations in relative peace, it had a ready supply of trained recruits who had fought in Afghanistan against the Soviet Union, and it had access to operatives like Mohammed Atta and the other 9/11 hijackers who were comfortable traveling in their target countries and had access to legal travel documents.[32] They were able to develop their organization to this extent because the U.S. government was focused at the time on state-sponsored terror and particularly on Iran, and did not realize the extent of the emerging threat.[33] U.S. security agencies are now extremely attuned to the possibility of another organization that looks like al Qaeda; the challenge will be adapting to an entity that has a completely different background and ideology but is attempting to develop similar capabilities.

These characteristics mean that market-state terrorism is not something that can be accepted as part of living in an open society, but in fact presents an existential challenge to open societies. The initial successes in responding to the threat of al Qaeda have produced a widespread impression that terrorism can be contained, and that the primary danger is in overreaction to a manageable threat. The fact that 18 years have passed without another attack on the scale of 9/11 despite the obvious strategic blunder of the Iraq War seems to strongly support this claim. This analysis works if three conditions are met: if al Qaeda was a unique case; if its successors can be identified and disrupted before they can plan and stage comparable attacks; and if weapons of mass destruction do not continue to proliferate and never end up in the hands of terrorist groups. If, however, al Qaeda is an early example of a new kind of terrorism, and future manifestations will appear in different and unpredictable forms that cannot be disrupted through drone strikes in the developing world, and weapons of mass destruction continue to proliferate, then the analysis leads to different conclusions.

Al Qaeda has been effectively disrupted in large part because our existing military capabilities match up very well to killing terrorists in the developing world but are much less well matched to other conceivable types of organizations operating domestically or in countries where drone strikes are not an option. Al Qaeda began in Egypt and Saudi Arabia as a nation-state terrorist organization but then evolved, but there is no reason to think that future threats will follow that path. They could come to our attention with a spectacular attack against the United States or other market-states without a long lead up period of being estranged from different host states while conducting smaller scale attacks.

Future market-state terrorist threats could appear in unfamiliar forms that sound almost silly today, like eco-terrorists or a millenarian cult—the specific ideology is less important than the characteristics that it be anti-modern and opposed to the market-state. The existential threat is not that market-state terrorists are going to take over a superpower state and start a world war, it is that terrorist groups with weapons of mass destruction don't need to take over a state in order to pose an existential threat to democracies.

One of the most disturbing possible models of this comes from the Japanese cult Aum Shinrikyo, which dispersed sarin gas on the Toyko subway in 1995 and killed 13 people.[34] This bizarre group, which initially focused on using yoga to develop psychic powers, gradually became apocalyptic and developed chemical and biological weapons programs and attempted multiple unsuccessful attacks employing botulinum, hydrogen cyanide (Zyklon B), and VX nerve agent before the subway attacks. They were largely unknown as they were developing their programs to obtain weapons of mass destruction, but when Japanese and American authorities investigated following the subway attacks they found the group had a 12-acre chemical weapons factory in Tokyo, an impressive staff of technical experts, $1 billion in resources, and a farm in Australia where it conducted experiments and gassed sheep. They even began a nuclear weapons program, purchasing land with uranium deposits in Australia and attempting to obtain mining licenses and purchasing equipment to this end in the United States.[35] A group with this level of resources and motivation operating with the benefit of the information on the internet and the advances in commercially available biotechnology that are available today could be much more successful in their efforts.

Antigovernment militia and white supremacist groups are a likely source of future attacks. A Government Accountability Office report in 2017 reported that 73 percent of terrorist deaths since 9/11 were from right-wing extremists.[36] Incidents like the massacre of Muslims in two New Zealand mosques in 2019 demonstrate that this type of terrorism is becoming increasingly internationalized and technology-enabled—the shooter streamed the attack live on Facebook and posted a manifesto online.[37] The deadliest terrorist attack perpetrated within the United States before 9/11 was the truck bombing of the Alfred P. Murrah Federal Building in Oklahoma City in 1995, an attack that killed 168 people and wounded hundreds more. The perpetrators, Timothy McVeigh and Terry Nichols, intended to challenge the legitimacy of the American government. Their ideology, a combination of survivalist militia and anger at the federal government, clearly fits within the framework of market-state terrorism. Terrorist attacks within the United States perpetrated by right-wing extremists have been consistently growing over the last decade,[38] and the number of militia groups in the United States has grown from 42 in 2008 to 276 in 2016, according to the Southern Poverty Law Center.[39]

These are ominous signs that indicate the threat will continue to increase and that larger terrorist attacks are likely.

We have a long experience with right-wing extremist terrorism in the United States, most dramatically in the form of the Ku Klux Klan, but this was fundamentally nation-state terrorism. A market-state version of the Ku Klux Klan could look very different—it would be decentralized, likely international, well funded, and focused on challenging the state directly through mass violence rather than using terrorist violence specifically to subjugate African Americans and other groups.

Organized Crime Will Not Recognize Limits

Organized crime has also been deeply affected by the nation-state to market-state transition. Nation-state organized crime exists as a parasitic copy of the state. It attempted to operate in secret, exercise illicit influence over senior government officials, and maximize the welfare of the members of the organization. There were strict limits in organizations like the Cosa Nostra on the activities that were tolerated by its members, and they avoided or restricted narcotics smuggling, focusing on the comparatively sustainable businesses of hijacking goods, loan-sharking, prostitution, gambling, and bookmaking.[40] There were limits on the use of violence, particularly activities that would bring large amounts of attention and pressure, such as killing journalists and law enforcement. The leaders of the organization were willing to forego some short-term profits for the long-term benefit of the organization and the well-being of its members. The iconic portrait of this worldview came in the movie *The Godfather*, which one senior Mafia member described in his memoir as a revelation for him and his counterparts.[41]

Market-state organized crime is undergoing an extremely dangerous evolution that parallels market-state terrorism. New criminal organizations, exemplified by the Mexican and Colombian drug cartels and Central American gangs, do not recognize the right of the state to limit their opportunities. Market-states also provide much larger and more lucrative markets for illicit products—this is shown by the massive growth of the drug market in the United States. The market for cocaine alone in the United States in recent decades has been estimated at tens of billions of dollars a year.[42] These organizations want to maximize the money they make and aggressively take risks to accomplish this, which are often directly in conflict with the welfare of members of the organization. Because they do not accept limitations on their opportunities, they will confront the state directly and challenge its legitimacy by directing violence against police and civilians. They also attempt to actively direct the public coverage of their activities, targeting uncooperative journalists directly, using theatrical violence to intimidate competitors and the government, and nearly always attempting to develop some kind of Robin Hood narrative to gain public support.

Criminal groups also increasingly have transnational corporate structures that include a presence in multiple countries, networked and decentralized organizations, and models to franchise out their criminal reputations. The franchise model is a particular parallel with market-state terrorism: drug smugglers attempting to establish themselves in a new region in Mexico will seek the Zetas brand in the same way that a new terrorist organization wants to be able to call itself part of al Qaeda.[43] Chapter 8 will discuss in detail how the existing law enforcement model is increasingly ill-suited to countering these organizations.

The influence and evolution of organized crime has been catalyzed by the alarming expansion of kleptocratic governments where leaders and their families control enormous portions of national wealth. These officials rely on illicit financial networks to conceal their wealth from the public and necessarily end up in symbiotic relationships with organized crime. The wealth that they conceal has reached astonishing levels. In 2012 the personal wealth of the seventy richest members of the Chinese national legislature was nearly $90 billion.[44] Russian president Vladimir Putin's personal fortune was credibly estimated in 2007 to be $40 billion.[45] This gives them enormous incentives to support the activities of illicit networks and makes them comfortable operating outside of legal and official channels, in a way that necessarily bleeds over into their official roles.

The question of exactly where organized crime ends and terrorism begins is tricky for homeland security practitioners, as the United States has developed a legal structure to confront modern terrorism that is based on the premise that terrorism is a different kind of threat from that posed by criminal organizations. As criminal groups adapt into a twenty-first-century form, however, it looks much more like a spectrum, and it is clear that criminal organizations such as the Colombian and Mexican drug cartels and Central American gangs have directly challenged the authority of the state to exert any control over their activities. They have also engaged in actions that are hard to accurately describe as anything other than terrorism: including blowing up civilian aircraft[46] (the Medellin cartel in Colombia in 1989) and burning down a crowded casino[47] (the Zetas in Mexico in 2011).

State-Based Challenges Will Increasingly Be Experienced as Homeland Security Threats

The connections between states and criminal or terrorist nonstate organizations are changing, and future state conflicts will also appear much more like a spectrum. This will give weaker states much greater flexibility. U.S. conventional military capabilities dwarf our state competitors, but this does not provide as much security as it used to. When major attacks cannot be immediately connected to responsible states, the deterrent effect of massive retaliation loses its power. Additionally, the possibility of escalating attacks from evolving nonstate actors makes preemption of every emergent threat an unviable strategy—security officials cannot possibly predict and intercept every new threat, particularly if it does not have the attributes of what they have experienced before. The ascendance of the market-state system, and in particular the dominant economic and military position of the United States, means that hostile states will increasingly rely on quasi-state entities and the use of proxies to challenge the United States and weapons of mass destruction to provide deterrence, rather than any kind of direct confrontation. This will exacerbate the homeland security challenges of confronting nonstate actors, as lines blur between state-sponsored groups, organized crime, and terrorist groups. The use of proxies and unofficial actors have some particular advantages for market-states, especially ones confronting a militarily and economically more powerful opponent.

Threats from other states will not focus on direct confrontation but on asymmetric attacks on the systems that support our lives. It has been frequently stated for decades that future conflict between states won't necessarily be acted out through direct conventional fighting. Two colonels in the Chinese People's Liberation Army wrote a book in 1999 called *Unrestricted Warfare* that describes the battlespace in twenty-first-century conflict as expanded to all aspects of a person's life.[48] The authors argue that in the nuclear age technological progress will no longer provide increasingly lethal weapons but instead opportunities to control, paralyze, and undermine opponents.[49] In this analysis the goal of warfare has changed from using force to impose your will to using every means to force the enemy to serve your interest—a very clear explanation of how state confrontations will change in the nation-state to market-state shift.[50]

The Particular Urgency of Weapons of Mass Destruction

The most alarming intersection of expanding technological capabilities, the incentives of weaker market-states, and evolving terrorist and organized crime groups is the proliferation of weapons of mass destruction. Increased proliferation of nuclear, radiological, biological, and chemical weapons in the coming decades is inevitable. This will be driven by the strong incentives for outsider states to develop and then increase their stockpiles of weapons of mass destruction, the technological advances that have vastly increased the capabilities of small laboratories, the growth in international clandestine networks to move goods and money within the legal systems of trade and finance, the increase in the availability of sensitive and previously closely guarded technical information, and the widespread availability of secure, immediate communications equipment.

Outsider states will continue to drive to obtain weapons of mass destruction for their own protection and to deter military action by more powerful states. Each time a new country succeeds, there is an increased incentive for rivals to develop their own weapons and a new potential source of proliferation. As states work to develop weapons of mass destruction, they develop networks with other outsider states and criminal smuggling organizations. This has been recently demonstrated dramatically by a UN report that showed that two shipments of chemical weapons between a North Korean company that has been blacklisted by the UN Security Council and the Syrian agency that oversees the country's chemical weapons development were intercepted in the first half of 2017.[51]

The perverse logic of proliferation is most clearly demonstrated by the career of the Pakistani metallurgist Abdul Qadeer Khan, who was almost single-handedly responsible for developing the Pakistani nuclear capability. Starting in 1975, he used expertise developed in and industrial secrets stolen from private company laboratories in the Netherlands to develop a capability to enrich uranium to the levels necessary for nuclear weapons. This knowledge led directly to Pakistan's development of a nuclear weapon in 1998. He then developed an international smuggling network of this technology to Iran, North Korea, and Libya, and was only stopped after American operatives intercepted cargo containers bound for Libya carrying equipment sent from his network in 2004.[52] This seeded the nuclear programs in North Korea, which had its first successful test in 2006, and Iran, which would likely have succeeded in developing its own capability if it had not been sabotaged by a cyber attack in 2010[53] and then subjected to international oversight as part of the 2015 Iran nuclear deal.[54]

Khan's network, which was backed by the Pakistani state but acted independently, engaged in proliferation activities apparently to expand its own influence and power.[55] Khan effectively operated a criminal proxy organization that did not always work in the interests of its state sponsor. While the Pakistani state surely did not want to be found to be smuggling nuclear technology to Libya, Khan's network had different incentives and acted accordingly. This demonstrates how quasi-state organizations within rogue states can act in unpredictable ways that have enormous consequences for other countries. It is likely that entities such as the Korea Mining Development Training Corporation, which was responsible for the previously mentioned smuggling of chemical weapons equipment to Syria, have complicated motivations based on the internal politics of North Korea, which may well cause them to act in ways that might not seem rational from outside. Therefore, as more countries obtain weapons of mass destruction, we have to expect that proliferation will continue to accelerate. Slowing this proliferation and eliminating smuggling networks is among the most urgent responsibilities of the developed world. The democratic world has become far, far too complacent by the success of the Cold War system of mutually assured destruction in preventing the use of a nuclear weapon against civilians over the last 75 years.

The most concerning possibility is of course that nuclear weapons could end up in the hands of a market-state terrorist group that would not hesitate to use them. Constructing a nuclear weapon is no longer a significant technical barrier: in 1977 a Princeton undergraduate was able to figure out how to build a simple bomb from publicly available material.[56] The fissile material necessary for a weapon—highly enriched uranium or plutonium about the size of a softball—is very difficult to obtain, however, which is the primary reason weapons have not proliferated further to this time.[57]

There is, however, a great deal of fissile material in the world and much of it is less safe than it should be. Approximately 3,200 tons of weapons grade material is distributed across 32 different countries,[58] which is sufficient for thousands of weapons. The vast majority of nuclear weapons and fissile material have always been in two countries, the United States and Russia, and in the latter the government collapsed and went from one state to 15 new states with nuclear weapons located in 14 of them. During this time organized crime, including arms dealers, became incredibly powerful, terrorist activity increased, and there has been significant military activity in places that had housed many of these weapons, like Ukraine and Georgia. Given this situation, there are reasons to be gravely concerned about the effectiveness of the controls that Russian authorities have been able to exercise on nuclear materials. As Graham Allison says, "Thefts of weapons-usable material and attempts to steal nuclear weapons are not a hypothetical possibility, but a proven fact." In 1997 the Russian general Alexander Lebed publicly acknowledged that 84 KGB "suitcase" nuclear bombs—devices between .1 and 1 kilotons that can be physically carried by a single person—were missing.[59] Though he publicly recanted and claimed implausibly that Russia had never made such weapons and even if they had they never would have lost them, the entire sequence was extremely alarming. The detonation of such a weapon in a populated city could cause tens of thousands of direct fatalities, many more horrifying injuries, and leave huge parts of the city uninhabitable.[†]

Terrorists are now actively working to obtain nuclear weapons, and market-state terrorist groups are not deterred by the prospect of massive retaliation. Osama bin Laden announced in 1998 that obtaining and deploying weapons of mass destruction was his religious duty, and he continued to work to obtain nuclear weapons for the rest of his life.[60] Bin Laden and his deputy Ayman al-Zawahiri received two former officials from Pakistan's nuclear program in August 2001.[61] A detailed essay on

---

† Anyone who would like to graphically understand the scale of the devastation as it would apply to cities around the world can visit https://nuclearsecrecy.com/nukemap/ and see this in visual form.

nuclear weapons found in the home of a senior al Qaeda official, along with other technical documents, led the nuclear weapons inspector David Albright to say that "Al Qaeda was intensifying its long-term goal to acquire nuclear weapons and would likely have succeeded, if it had remained powerful in Afghanistan for several more years."[62] Separatist Chechen terrorists have also been long interested in nuclear materials, and in 1995 a group placed a simple radiological dispersal device (a "dirty" bomb that would spread radiation from a conventional rather than a nuclear explosion) in a Moscow park, although they did not subsequently detonate it.[63]

Biological weapons generally receive less attention than nuclear bombs but are potentially even more concerning, because the technology is advancing so quickly, the resources required to create a potentially devastating weapon are much less, and it is much easier to hide biological weapon development within the activities of a legitimate laboratory than it is to conceal the enrichment of nuclear material. These weapons are certain to further proliferate, driven by remarkable recent advances in biomedical technology. The cost of assembling complex DNA sequences is dropping rapidly and synthesizing deadly viruses no longer requires institutional laboratories.[64] Terrorists could develop much more advanced capabilities than was possible previously, and a group as well-resourced as al Qaeda was before 9/11 or Aum Shinrikyo in the early 1990s operating today would surely make much more rapid progress on developing biological weapons. We're reaching a point where any competent biologist with DNA synthesis skills can create a disease like smallpox or experiment to develop novel and possibly disastrous variations on existing diseases.[65]

More and more potentially sensitive information is now publicly available, and it is very likely that this information will be used by terrorist groups to stage potentially catastrophic attacks. In a notorious recent example, Canadian researchers published a paper showing in painstaking detail how they assembled a smallpox-like virus using commercially available DNA samples ordered over the internet.[66] The availability of this kind of information can only be expected to continue to increase. The introduction raised the question of the U.S. government's preparedness for unexpected outbreaks, and it is clear that a weaponized virus could quickly cause mass panic and overwhelm response capabilities.

Migration Crises Are Much More Immediate

The United States and other wealthy countries will experience increasing flows of migrants and asylum seekers through nontraditional routes. This will be further driven by the increases in severe weather events and natural disasters around the world. The United States is already seeing this: apprehensions of non-Mexicans are now greater than apprehensions of Mexicans, and other populations such as Indian or Cuban nationals are no longer a rarity on the Southwest land border. The flows of Syrian nationals throughout Europe show how the use of terror against civilians in one country can quickly create a migration crisis thousands of miles away, and how developed countries will increasingly deal with refugees at their borders instead of processing them remotely. Transnational criminal organizations make enormous amounts of money moving desperate people through increasingly complex travel routes. The international systems to process refugees are all based on this idea that international organizations and aid groups go to places where disaster has struck and process refugees there and then relocate them—this is increasingly being overtaken by the refugees themselves. This will be discussed in more detail in chapter 6.

Natural Disasters Are Getting Worse

In the United States the question of whether human activity has caused increases in global temperatures has bizarrely become a partisan political issue, with President Trump and leading members of the Republican Party publicly deriding the notion that change is occurring.[67] From a homeland security perspective, the objections of the Republican Party to the change are beside the point. The key issue is that temperatures are quantifiably changing, and that changes in climate, whatever the cause, result in unpredictable and dangerous increases in severe weather. The implications of this are clear: there will be a series of escalating natural disasters in coming years, and the impact of these disasters will be magnified by the increased concentration of people in urban locations.

When climate change has occurred in the past, as it did in the seventeenth century when temperatures suddenly cooled, the effect on human societies was devastating. In his book *Global Crisis*, the historian Geoffrey Parker traces the effect of abnormally cold temperatures in the mid-seventeenth century and demonstrates that *up to a third of the worldwide human population died* in the disasters and wars that were driven by this change. Temperatures between 1640 and 1690 were so abnormally cold that the period has been called the Little Ice Age by climatologists. The most alarming conclusions of the book are that climate change can occur extremely quickly, and that human societies have historically always been unprepared for the changes that occur in these situations. As Parker argues:

> The current debate on "global warming" confuses two issues: whether human activity is making the world warmer; and whether or not sudden climate change can occur. Although some may still legitimately question the first, the seventeenth-century evidence places the second beyond doubt. The critical issues are not *whether* climate change occurs, but *when*; and whether it makes better sense for states and societies to invest money now to prepare for natural disasters that are inevitable—hurricanes in the Gulf and Atlantic coasts of North America; storm surges in the lands around the North Sea; droughts in Africa; prolonged heatwaves—or instead wait to pay the far higher costs of inaction.[68]

Whatever you believe has caused the recent change, the fact is that temperatures have increased in recent decades and appear to be continuing. The National Oceanic and Atmospheric Association describes the changes that have occurred clearly:[69]

> Though warming has not been uniform across the planet, the upward trend in the globally averaged temperature shows that more areas are warming than cooling. Since 1880, surface temperature has risen at an average pace of 0.13°F (0.07°C) every 10 years for a net warming of 1.69°F (0.94°C) through 2016. Over this 137-year period, average temperature over land areas has warmed faster than ocean temperatures: 0.18°F (0.10°C) per decade compared to 0.11°F (0.06°C) per decade. The last year with a temperature cooler than the twentieth-century average was 1976.

This has driven an increase in the number of severe weather events experienced around the world. The effects of temperature shifts on weather patterns extend beyond what is intuitively obvious: as an example in the seventeenth century, reductions in global temperatures caused a much higher number of El Niño events (when the normal pattern of winds blowing east from the Americas to Asia is reversed) than normal. This caused weaker than normal monsoons in Asia that devastated harvests, widespread flooding in the Americas, and, likely, a large increase in volcanic eruptions around the Pacific. This increase in volcanic activity was probably because of a shift in sea levels—usually the Pacific is 24 inches higher in Asia than in America, which reverses in El Niño years. This causes a huge change in the pressure on the tectonic plates throughout the Pacific region.[70] The key point is that climate changes, in any direction, exacerbate severe weather in unpredictable and dangerous ways.

The impact of the severe weather changes has clearly already begun. A review in the *Bulletin of the American Meteorological Society* of 27 severe weather events in 2016 determined that climate change was a "significant driver" in 21 of them.[71] A report by the World Meteorological Organization in 2014 analyzed natural disasters between 1970 and 2012 and found that they were occurring *five times* as frequently in the last decade as in the 1970s.[72] Increasingly severe weather, combined with greater urbanization and some of the other trends that have been discussed, will have major effects on the scale of the disasters that American society and the world face in coming years.

2 | The Implications of New Vulnerabilities

The previous chapter argued that national security threats no longer occur internationally, and that technological changes, expanding nonstate or indirect state-backed threats, and the continued proliferation of weapons of mass destruction require a new strategic approach. This chapter describes some of the areas that will require much greater focus, why reorganizations are so difficult, how to manage the process of adaptation with a particular emphasis on privacy, and addresses some of the reasons the political discussion about these issues is so misleading and useless.

Certain activities are becoming much more important due to the shifts identified in the previous chapter. The first and most obvious is the need for a counterterrorism approach that intervenes to disrupt terrorist groups and prevents trained terrorist operatives from exploiting legal travel, trade, and financial networks to prepare and execute attacks. Market-state terrorist organizations like al Qaeda have demonstrated themselves to be too dangerous for the twentieth-century process of investigation and prosecution. This adaptation is underway and includes a much greater focus on gathering and disseminating information about known and suspected terrorists, integrating this information with border controls, and on international financial movements.

This emphasis on disrupting organizations and closing vulnerabilities will also increasingly apply to efforts to counter organized crime. Law enforcement will be driven to shift from a greater emphasis on long-term investigations to a focus on denying criminal organizations the ability to operate. If crimes are being committed by decentralized networks in areas where U.S. law enforcement has limited jurisdiction, it doesn't make sense to spend years trying to build a case against a kingpin; the focus needs to be on stopping the activity. This will also mean that law enforcement and national security will be blended in a way that has previously been intentionally avoided, as transnational groups and quasi-state actors are able to commit crimes and move money across jurisdictions.

In addition to recognizing emergent market-state terrorist organizations and denying them the infrastructure and ability to operate, it is also essential to prepare for unanticipated threats by identifying and closing vulnerabilities, and particularly by expanding capabilities to protect civilians during and after attacks and disasters on a greater scale than the United States has previously experienced domestically. The response capabilities and institutions that we organized in the twentieth century are built on the assumption that military attacks from hostile states pose the only potential existential threats, and built into this assumption is the idea that only a massive military response can deter them. Planning to respond to terrorist weapons of mass destruction is different: the military response capabilities would not deter the initial strike and in the aftermath of an attack attribution could be extremely difficult. For a potential biological weapon, like a particularly virulent new strain of influenza, it might be unclear for a very long time whether the devastation was caused intentionally or who could have done so.

Planning for a state-based nuclear strike and a terrorist weapon of mass destruction are fundamentally different things. State-based planning assumes that devastation would overwhelm any conceivable emergency response and that the focus would be on command and control for counterstrikes. This is certainly rational, because it is estimated that 90 percent of the U.S. population would be killed in a major nuclear exchange.[1] A terrorist attack or multiple attacks using weapons of mass destruction would demand a different type of response, one that could actually be planned for even if the situation would be horrifying. There would be a massive need for field hospitals and medical emergency response deployed domestically; supplies of food, water, and power; and huge amounts of transportation and shelter for displaced people as existing systems would be overwhelmed. Quickly deploying sufficient law enforcement to maintain order in devastated areas would be essential to prevent looting and other kinds of crime. There would also be an overwhelmingly urgent need to prevent any additional weapons or attackers from entering the country or reloading another attack from within the country. Increasingly, effective response to disasters will require expenditures of effort that we normally only associate with military operations or rescues in the financial sector.

The public and private sectors will need to work together on security planning to close vulnerabilities much more extensively than in the past. The current system, based on voluntary compliance and limited information sharing, is inadequate. An example of that is when an urgent threat to privately owned critical infrastructure is identified through classified means, but officials are unable to communicate this information to the private owners of the infrastructure asset unless they can find someone with a security clearance or find a way to transmit the key points in a declassified form. Both of these courses of action create communications delays that are increasingly unacceptable in the face of twenty-first-century threats. A main result of this, though, will be to establish much greater security requirements for private sector companies, vastly expanded information sharing between government and industry, and significant new security costs for companies.

There is an urgent need for international venues to address nonstate threats beyond the nation-state-centered world of the United Nations. Most of the existing international structures to deal with things like weapons of mass destruction are entirely focused on weapons developed by states. The international treaty addressing biological weapons, the Biological Weapons Convention, was established in 1975 and is entirely focused on preventing governments from developing biological weapons with no capacity to address nonstate actors.[2] This is wildly inadequate in a world where small laboratories can develop weapons that would have required the resources of a nation-state in the 1970s. The international framework for refugees and migrants is structured to handle displaced people who have been persecuted by a state because of their membership in a certain group (e.g., ethnic, political, religious), and is poorly suited to helping vulnerable people who have not been displaced, are victimized by gangs or criminal organizations, or who do not meet the category of persecuted groups.

The new threats identified here do not mean that multilateral work is less important or that the United States should disengage. On the contrary, it makes it more urgent for the United States and other market-states to work together to provide security for civilians and to develop useful structures to do so. Protecting civilians around the world is increasingly important because disorders reverberate much more quickly than they ever did previously. Humanitarian assistance also has an essential role in building goodwill toward the United States and countering the propaganda of terrorist organizations. Partnerships with neighboring countries where populations are integrated and move back and forth across borders will continue to increase in importance as well. For the United States this means increasingly deep engagement with Canada and Mexico to address shared problems.

Privacy

A much better privacy balance needs to be established that meets security requirements but provides a predictable and tolerable level of protection to individuals from intrusive activities by government or companies. The modern privacy regime, and the public argument about it, is based on a framework that was created to address activities like phone tapping and intelligence agencies gathering information about American citizens during the Cold War,[3] and has been outpaced by technological developments. The result is that there are bright lines about the activities that government can conduct that don't match the most pressing concerns for citizens. As an example, there is generally a great deal of media attention to anything DHS does related to social media, even if it involves information that is posted publicly. CBP's ability to search the content of electronic devices including phones and laptops at the border, on the other hand, has been settled in court and receives comparatively less attention, despite being something that most people would find more concerning than looking at their LinkedIn profile. Private companies, meanwhile, are conducting staggeringly invasive activities and selling incredibly sensitive information. A *New York Times* investigation in 2018 discovered at least 75 companies that were collecting and selling incredibly precise information about people's movements from smartphone applications whose ostensible purpose was providing weather updates or local news.[4]

To provide an appropriate balance in the new security environment, new trade-offs will have to be established. The basis of the new approach should be this: *People will need to accept, and are in many cases already accepting, reduced levels of privacy when traveling, moving goods, engaging in significant financial transactions, and purchasing weapons or weapons components. There should in turn be, however, much higher standards for collecting, storing, and disseminating personal information, whether by government or industry.*

These kinds of changes are already in place for travelers, as will be discussed in detail in chapter 5, but briefly authorities need to know who or what is coming before it arrives, be able to compare that information to preestablished lists of potentially dangerous individuals and companies they are connected to, and then verify that the people or goods that arrive are who or what they claim to be. This is accomplished by collecting certain advance information, maintaining watch lists, and collecting passenger biometrics to match individuals to identities.

The authorities that law enforcement entities are able to exercise when someone crosses the border are much greater than what would be allowed in any domestic situation. An individual can be questioned and searched based on the standard of "reasonable suspicion," which is less stringent than "probable cause." The Supreme Court has also repeatedly upheld the right of the Border Patrol to do immigration inspections at interior checkpoints on major roads in the border region.[5]

There has been significant initial resistance to increased data collection about travelers internationally. Privacy concerns have been the primary obstacle to closer coordination with the European Union, and to a lesser extent Canada, on targeting and information sharing about known and suspected terrorists. Privacy advocates and European officials were unanimously and strongly opposed to the U.S. government collection of airline reservation data and initially would not allow it to be shared beyond CBP.[6] DHS and its European Union counterparts have gone through a number of laborious negotiations over whether the United States can require European air carriers to collect information about European citizens that could violate some of their existing privacy protections. Most of these focus on the possibility of information that is collected for one purpose being used for an additional purpose (which is nearly always a counterterrorism investigation). These have now been resolved, but only in some instances through legislative changes in the European Union and the establishment of stringent protections for the data by the U.S. government. After the 2015 Paris terror attacks it became clear the European Union did not have effective systems to track foreign fighters returning from Syria, and they put their own system to collect airline reservation data in place.[7]

When appropriate trade-offs have not been made, the push to provide sufficient security tends to mean high levels of privacy in certain areas accompanied by major overreach in others. This is dramatically shown by the measures that are being taken to provide security at American schools in response to appalling numbers of school shootings. Gun rights groups like the National Rifle Association advocate, and have been able to legislatively obtain, an extreme level of privacy for individuals who want to purchase firearms. This is based on the belief that the Second Amendment affords unique protections around firearms that go far beyond the Fourth Amendment protections from unreasonable search and seizure that form the basis for other privacy rights. Their position is genuinely radical. In September 2019, in response to a mass shooting in Odessa, Texas, the lieutenant governor and the National Rifle Association engaged in a public argument over whether an individual should have to go through a background check before they can purchase an assault rifle from a stranger (as the shooter did), which wouldn't even apply if the seller knows the purchaser.[8] Because the level of violence driven by the widespread availability of weapons is intolerable, however, schools and authorities are taking extremely invasive actions in other areas. Students are subject to locker checks and may be required to wear clear backpacks, to participate in drills that prepare them to respond to the experience of being massacred by an armed classmate, and have their social media activities monitored closely by authorities.[9]

The technology industry is currently driving some of the most egregious privacy imbalances. The traditional expectations of privacy that citizens have had in their daily lives have been completely superseded by technology. In the twentieth century, a civilian could be confident that their private correspondence, conversations, and physical movements could only be tracked legally by law enforcement agencies meeting a reviewable judicial standard.

Public outcry often focuses on when this is used by law enforcement to circumvent protections. The judicial "third-party doctrine" holds that individuals do not have an expectation of privacy when they share data with third parties, which clearly is poorly matched to a situation in which people carry phones with data harvesting applications everywhere they go. In 2018 the Supreme Court held that law enforcement could not obtain location information from cellular sites without a warrant, and similar updates to existing doctrine to match technological changes will likely progress.[10]

Law enforcement using these applications to circumvent existing controls is alarming. What is much more alarming is that this information, once collected, can be breached by hostile actors like foreign intelligence agencies, criminal organizations, or terrorists. It's not reasonable to expect that a location tracking company that lacks the internal controls to keep their services from being used by stalkers in defiance of court orders[11] to keep, say, a terrorist organization from tracking the movements of members of the military or their families.

The staggering inability of industry to prevent these abuses makes a regulatory reckoning inevitable—their behavior is demanding major government action and making catastrophes that will generate enormous public outcry inevitable. Privacy is going to have to be integrated into the development of new technologies, and controls will need to be enforced by a corresponding level of regulation.

Outdated Frameworks Lead to Bad Decisions

The opposition of European Union officials and privacy advocates to the collection of airline reservation data by DHS shows how new security challenges cause particular strain for officials with outdated paradigms. People who rely on twentieth-century frameworks to respond to market-state security challenges will struggle to make balanced decisions: everything that an agency like DHS does looks like some kind of awful overreach and militarization of domestic life. Conversely, approaches that fit within previous frameworks will seem extremely appealing even if they are very poorly suited to the problem at hand—in particular, trying to find military solutions to homeland security problems.

This has been vividly demonstrated by the Trump administration's attempts to limit migration on the Southwest border. Despite having campaigned on building a wall along the Southwest border and ending illegal migration, President Trump has actually presided over a major increase in illegal border crossings, with Fiscal Year 2019 levels of apprehensions the highest in a dozen years.[12] This actually understates the scale of the failure, since in the early 2000s many of the crossers were Mexican migrants who would be apprehended multiple times over the course of the year in different attempts to cross, while in 2019 the majority of people arriving are Central American asylum seekers. This means that many more unique individuals were succeeding in illegally crossing the border under President Trump than under his predecessors.

President Trump has attempted to respond to twenty-first-century migration with the tactics of a twentieth-century nationalist: building a physical wall and inflicting hardship on individual migrants. When this failed he told the military to build the wall and sent troops to the border, where they spent their time putting up largely cosmetic security features or painting the existing fencing since the military is not legally able to enforce immigration laws.[13] Despite the administration's willingness to take appalling actions, like separating families, they were ineffective at their main objective. This shows what happens when leaders have a fundamental misunderstanding of the strategic context: if decisionmakers are trying to apply 1950s solutions to 2019 they will simply fail, no matter how cruel or extreme they are willing to be. After the disastrous summer of 2019 even the Trump administration changed course, which is clearly demonstrated by the president's pivot to focusing on forcing migrants to remain in Mexico and Central America through so-called "safe third country agreements" and increasing Mexican enforcement efforts through tariff threats while using redirected military funds to build symbolic sections of the promised wall.

The Political Discussion of Homeland Security Is Harmful and Seems to Be Getting Worse

The political discussion about how to protect citizens and their interests is particularly detached and unhelpful at a time when urgent decisions about resources, strategy, legal regimes, and constantly increasing vulnerabilities are unaddressed. The situation would be less alarming if the American national security establishment had a framework in place to make effective decisions about preventing and responding to twenty-first-century threats. It does not.

The distorted political discussion didn't begin with President Trump, although he has certainly made things worse. This was exemplified by an earlier manifestation of the migration crisis that I dealt with extensively while in government: the flows of unaccompanied Central American children that arrived in south Texas in record numbers beginning in 2012 and putting an enormous strain on the immigration processing system in 2014. This was driven largely by a 2008 legal change that ensured that any unaccompanied children from noncontiguous countries apprehended at the border (essentially any non-Mexican children) would be immediately transferred into the custody of the Department of Health and Human Services and put into whichever situation is in the best interest of the child while they go through immigration court processing, which often means they are placed with family members who are in the country illegally.

There were important questions raised by this crisis. These included (1) whether it was appropriate to continue the 2008 law or whether it should be reevaluated, (2) whether our existing refugee and asylum laws were adequate to cover people fleeing violence from gangs that effectively controlled their communities, and (3) whether the interior institutions for processing migrants, including the Health and Human Services' refugee processing organization, Immigration and Customs Enforcement (ICE) removal operations, and the Department of Justice's immigration courts, are adequate and effective, and if not how they should be changed to efficiently deal with migration flows that are qualitatively different from what has been seen in the past.

Instead, the public discussion about Central American migration addressed none of these urgent issues and focused on questions that had little bearing on the actual events. Rick Perry, the governor of Texas, attempted to call in the National Guard in response to the influx of unaccompanied children and families. Given that children were presenting themselves to Border Patrol agents to trigger the legal protections that began once they were apprehended, sending National Guard members to assist in interdictions was bizarrely detached from the actual problems.

On the other side of the issue, in December 2015 it was leaked to the press that Homeland Security was planning a series of "raids" to remove Central American families.[14] This turned out to be removals of families who had been apprehended crossing the border illegally after 2014, who had been through the full immigration court process (taking months or years), who had exhausted any claims to humanitarian protections including refugee status, and who had received final orders of removal from an immigration judge. This was completely in keeping with the law and ICE's standard practice, just on a slightly larger scale than normal.

The operations resulted in 78 individuals being removed in January 2016, as compared to the 40 or so who were being removed each month up to that point. There certainly may be issues with the processing that individuals receive in immigration court or the ways in which their removals were effected. Characterizing these removals as indiscriminate raids, however, was extremely misleading. Amazingly, both of the Democratic presidential candidates at the time, Hillary Clinton and Bernie Sanders, endorsed the position that none of these Central Americans should be removed at all, even if they had been found to not meet the requirements of refugee status, been ordered removed by an immigration judge, and had no legal basis to stay in the country.

The language about raids brought back visceral memories of sudden enforcement actions affecting migrants in certain locations in a seemingly arbitrary manner, for example in Operation Wagon Train, when in 2006 ICE agents detained 1,300 workers at six Swift & Company meatpacking plants throughout the Midwest, many of whom were later deported. The actions taken by the Obama administration in 2015 were simply different from this. Calling them raids obscured what was actually happening and the very important point that the position of most of the advocacy organizations and the two leading Democratic candidates was that there should be essentially no enforcement of immigration laws for Central Americans, who now cross the Southwest border in greater numbers than Mexicans do. The political environment in which important homeland security topics are discussed was completely divorced from the facts of the situation.

3 | The Unpleasant Process of Reorganizing a Government

The events of 9/11 and the enormous changes that were required afterward showed how poorly prepared the U.S. government was to protect civilians from twenty-first-century terrorism. We have now adapted and are much better prepared to respond to al Qaeda and similar organizations, but significant vulnerabilities are growing in other areas. This shows how mismatched our strategy and resources can be to different emerging threats and how difficult it will be to adapt. Despite major increases in the DHS budget, investment in security abroad continues to dwarf the effort and spending on domestic security and response capabilities—the 2019 DHS budget request is about 10 percent of the Defense budget, and significant additional international efforts move through State and the Intelligence Community.[1]

Reorganizing government is very difficult, and necessarily means confronting major entrenched interests and causing significant disruption to existing processes. This disruption creates significant openings for fraud and makes duplication and waste more likely, as new oversight and management structures need to be developed. The comparative lack of oversight can also lead to significant overreach and abuses by officials. New agencies, or existing agencies performing new functions, are frequently less competent than established organizations and frustrate their counterparts. Reorganizations create openings for opportunists in government to try to get unmerited promotion, while at the same time established agencies may take the opportunity to offload incompetent staff or to get rid of unwanted functions, further damaging the competence of the new organization. Finally, the political environment surrounding reorganizations, which are necessarily driven by government failures, creates openings for the most cynical kind of political exploitation.

These challenges were exemplified by the last major reorganization of the U.S. government beginning with the National Security Act of 1947,[2] which unified the American military agencies within the Department of Defense and enabled forward deployed troops around the world, massively increased intelligence spending and established the CIA, and created the NSC as a coordinating mechanism across security agencies. This was followed in 1953 by the establishment of the National Security Agency (NSA) to further expand intelligence collection.[3] At the same time, the ascent of federal law enforcement that began during the 1930s "War on Crime" continued until the FBI became the preeminent American law enforcement agency.[4] This reorganization developed into the familiar system with which the United States ended the twentieth century, with clear lines between domestic law enforcement and international military, foreign policy, and intelligence functions.

Strategically, this reorganized security structure was successful, and it achieved its objective of winning the Cold War while largely avoiding intolerable domestic repression. The process, though, took decades and was filled with setbacks and problems. The deficiencies of the new structure were made glaringly obvious by the Vietnam War and the Defense Department had so much difficulty unifying its command structures that it needed to be reorganized again through the Goldwater-Nichols Act in 1986,[5] which established combatant commanders reporting directly to the secretary of defense. It is worth emphasizing that this correction occurred a full 39 years after the new department was established.

There were also major intelligence and law enforcement abuses. The CIA's enthusiastic work to kill foreign leaders, which led Lyndon Johnson to remark after becoming president that the government "had been operating a damned Murder Inc. in the Caribbean,"[6] was revealed publicly and led to an executive order in 1976 forbidding any U.S. government employee from engaging or conspiring in political assassinations.[7] In 1975, a Senate Select Committee that became known as the Church Committee (after its chairman, Senator Frank Church) identified egregious domestic spying by the FBI, CIA, and NSA on antiwar and civil rights activists, and led to the Foreign Intelligence Surveillance Act (FISA), which established a separate judicial review process for wiretaps and surveillance involving American citizens.[8]

As the U.S. government was reorienting to deal with the challenges of the Cold War, the process was made much more difficult by some of the most infamous political exploitation in American history. After the Communist Party–led revolution in China, Senator Joseph McCarthy, who had been looking for an issue to bring himself to national prominence, seized the opportunity to charge that hundreds of State Department employees were secret members of the U.S. Communist Party and then spent four years escalating his allegations before he was finally discredited and disgraced.[9] Among the many awful things about this period in American history, it led directly to a very real purge of the government's most experienced experts on Asia, right as the decisions were being made that led to increased commitments to war in Vietnam.

Creating DHS

The origins of DHS were as messy as this historical precedent would indicate. After the 9/11 attacks it was clear that the problems of coordination between the different agencies with responsibility for preventing terrorist attacks were such that a major reorganization needed to take place. Information sharing continued to be a major challenge and many departments were continuing to conduct business as usual. This was astonishingly demonstrated when the Immigration and Naturalization Service approved and sent visas to two of the 9/11 hijackers six months after their deaths in the attack.[10]

After initially opposing the idea, President George W. Bush publicly announced on June 6, 2002 that he was asking Congress to create a new department to oversee homeland security functions. The Department of Homeland Security was established on November 25, 2002, and on March 1, 2003 the department incorporated 22 different entities from across the government, including from Justice, Treasury, Agriculture, Transportation, the General Services Administration, Health and Human Services, Energy, and Defense.* Tom Ridge, a former Pennsylvania governor and President Bush's top advisor on homeland security at the White House, became the first secretary.

As is made clear by the time between President Bush's public announcement and the time that the department became operational, DHS was created extremely quickly as a direct response to the 9/11 attacks, and it is

---

* The full list is available here: https://www.Homeland Security.gov/who-joined-Homeland Security

important to remember that the decisions that have defined the department were made in a crisis atmosphere and through frantic congressional horse-trading. Few things happen quickly in government, and establishing an entirely new cabinet agency is generally not one of them. This inevitably resulted in a structure that is likely not what anyone would have intentionally designed for the department, but rather what was able to be agreed upon in a very short amount of time under extreme pressure. Even the headquarters was found and occupied on the fly, in a former boarding school that had been taken over by the Navy during the Second World War. As a result, the secretary of homeland security currently occupies an office that is significantly more modest than that of an average deputy assistant secretary in more established departments.

Some of the decisions about what was included in DHS still provoke particular head scratching. The new department centralized immigration and border control functions but did not include the immigration courts, which remained at the Department of Justice, or visa issuance, which stayed with the State Department's Consular Affairs office. Initially, several components of Health and Human Services, which handle disease response and refugee resettlement, were going to be included but removed after forceful lobbying by the secretary at the time.[11] DHS included the Coast Guard and the Federal Emergency Management Agency (FEMA) but not the National Guard, which is deployed in response to disasters domestically. For a department created specifically in response to 9/11, it left out many of the entities most relevant to the attacks. The Secret Service was included but not the CIA or FBI, which were the primary counterterrorist organizations at the time. The Federal Aviation Administration, which had a major role in issuing ground stops on the day of the attacks, remains in the Department of Transportation. The new department also conspicuously did not include the newly formed Terrorist Screening Center and National Counterterrorism Center.[12]

DHS was conceived to fulfill a role similar to that of a typical interior[†] ministry or the United Kingdom's home secretary. Unlike most interior ministries, however, it does not contain the key counterterrorism functions in the U.S. government, which are within the Intelligence Commu-

---

† The United States does of course have a Department of the Interior, but it is an outlier in that it focuses on public lands and natural resources and has a minimal security function.

nity and primarily the CIA for international counterterrorism efforts, and within the FBI in the Department of Justice for domestic investigation and prosecution of terrorism cases. Most of DHS's actual counterterrorism work is specifically related to travel or international commerce, and it is led by the several hundred officials at CBP's National Targeting Center who identify watch-listed people or things before they can come into the United States. DHS also has an important supporting role to the FBI through participation in the interagency Joint Terrorism Task Forces, which are located around the country. The FBI's counterterrorism responsibilities after 9/11 have shifted resources and attention away from other responsibilities, such as public corruption, countering organized crime, and human smuggling and trafficking.

In effect, because of the different agencies involved and interlocking authorities, counterterrorism efforts are coordinated by the National Security Council, in particular the Counterterrorism Security Group meetings that were started before 9/11 and have expanded to include all of the key law enforcement and intelligence agencies. In international engagements, DHS tends to be matched up with interior ministries, although nearly all other interior ministries include the federal police force charged with counterterrorism.

While DHS has not consolidated the counterterrorism roles, it has improved the existing coordination problems in other areas. It includes the national customs authority as part of CBP, which gives the department expansive authorities that are beyond those of most interior ministries. In most other countries the customs authorities are kept in the finance ministry (where they were in the United States before 2003, as part of Treasury), while migration enforcement resides in the interior ministry. This creates an obvious disconnect between the two agencies, which are both responsible for monitoring the movement of people into and out of the country. Every U.S. port of entry used to have three different port directors, one from the Customs Service, one from the Immigration and Naturalization Service, and one from the Department of Agriculture. By establishing a unified border control agency in CBP, Homeland Security significantly streamlined border processing and created the possibility of important security gains by eliminating coordination problems.

At the same time as DHS created a single face at the border handling customs, immigration, and most agricultural inspections, however, it created a new and unusual coordination problem by separating out the investigative and interdiction functions into two different agencies, ICE and CBP, respectively. Both legacy Customs and the Immigration and Naturalization Service had inspectors and investigators within the same agency. Practically no major police department separates detectives and beat cops into entirely different agencies, and the result of this is that there is ongoing tension between the leadership of the two agencies and coordination problems that would be avoided if they were combined.

It is also important to emphasize how DHS is an extremely young department when examining its structure and management issues. Everyone understands this conceptually, but it is very easy to forget when watching the department operate in real time. As an example, I would hear constant complaints from colleagues at the White House about DHS and the disorganization of its officials as they explicitly compared it to other entities like the Department of State, which has existed with a continuous and focused mission since 1789. These criticisms are unfair; it is exceptionally difficult for any individual to represent the diverse operational components of DHS and their sometimes competing interests, especially when they still are not used to having to coordinate and work together on crosscutting issues.

As DHS asserts itself it constantly comes into conflict with established departments, who resent what they see as an intrusion on their bureaucratic territory and try to restrain DHS's activities. The DHS memoirs of people like Tom Ridge, the first DHS secretary, and Stewart Baker, the DHS assistant secretary for policy from 2005 to 2009, are filled with stories of bureaucratic conflict and frustration.

As Baker describes the relationship with State:

From the moment of its creation, DHS has been State's adversary. At the outset, State barely prevented Congress from transferring its consular service to the new department locks, stock, and barrel. And we were constantly complicating State's diplomacy, either demanding more of foreign nations on the security front or sending their most prominent citizens to hard-nosed secondary inspection on the border.[13]

And as Ridge describes the FBI's unwillingness to share information with DHS:

Even so, I would occasionally get blindsided at my daily morning meetings with the president. He would ask about something that he'd learned from the FBI and often I hadn't a clue what he was talking about. It's not a good strategy for the secretary of homeland security to say in response "I am unaware of it, Mr. President." At least, not very often.[14]

Homeland Security outside of DHS

Large parts of the federal homeland security enterprise are outside of DHS. The White House is the central coordinator for all homeland security issues. Prior to 9/11, a senior director in the National Security Council led the Counterterrorism Security Group, which involved the FBI, CIA, Customs, the Immigration and Naturalization Service, and other interested agencies. President Bush created a Homeland Security Council (HSC) in 2003 to mirror the NSC, overseen by an assistant to the president for homeland security and counterterrorism. The NSC primarily convenes executives across the national security agencies for decision-making meetings, and the staff of the NSC focuses on preparing and developing policy issues for decisions by executives. The HSC replicated these functions for homeland security issues. The lack of a clear demarcation between homeland security and national security issues meant that this structure caused difficult coordination issues. Additionally, the NSC staff is made up of staff detailed from different agencies and the established national security agencies like State, the CIA, and Defense are heavily represented. This means that NSC staff generally dislike having to deal with DHS, which they see as encroaching on their turf. As a result, the HSC staff were seen by the NSC staff as a de facto liaison to DHS, which is both unpleasant for the HSC staff and makes DHS an afterthought in NSC policymaking. This nearly always leads to problems. DHS ends up needing to be involved in all sorts of different national security policy decisions, and delaying their engagement or relaying messages just ensures the process won't go well.

President Barack Obama combined both entities into a joint NSC, so that the former Homeland Security Council reported to the national security advisor through the assistant to the president for homeland security and counterterrorism who was also a deputy national security advisor (if that seems confusing to you, rest assured that it is also confusing to the staff involved). The effect of this was that counterterrorism was elevated to the same level of attention as top national security concerns, but other homeland security issues were not unless a disaster was actively occurring. President Trump initially announced that the two councils would be split again, but the subsequent disorganization and centralization of decision-making outside of the NSC process seems to have overtaken that announcement. The NSC remains the place where any issues involving complicated coordination or disagreements between departments are worked through, and its role in homeland security has expanded significantly in recent years.

The NSC is always a popular place to put major problems. This is because a senior NSC official will be able to elevate issues to the president regularly, which is the most effective way to overcome resistance and force government agencies to do things that they might not otherwise be willing to do. This approach was shown clearly by the appointment of the Ebola Czar, discussed in the introduction, and it is likely that crises will continue to be handled this way since officials outside of the White House structure lack the ability to quickly elevate decisions across the government. The limitation is that it relies on the president's time and attention, which is always the most valuable commodity in Washington.

The Domestic Policy Council has had particular influence on immigration and border security in the Obama and Trump administrations. In the Obama administration the Domestic Policy Council led the development of the executive actions on immigration enforcement, and the role of Domestic Policy Advisor Steven Miller in the Trump administration's reduction of refugee admissions and other policies is widely acknowledged.[15] The Office of Management and Budget also has an underappreciated but crucial role in the homeland security enterprise. Because of its control over the budget and oversight of departments and agencies, and because unlike the rest of the White House it is largely staffed by career experts who remain in place while political leadership changes, this is the White House office with the deepest institutional knowledge of the homeland security enterprise and an extremely important ability to influence the structure and development of the federal institutions involved.

The role of the Department of Defense in homeland security is comparatively opaque and contentious. The department's mission, "to provide the military forces needed to deter war and to protect the security of our country," is fundamentally focused on military threats from foreign countries. At the same time, the department has by far the most resources and largest capabilities in the federal government, so presidents are always tempted to turn to them when homeland security problems seem overwhelming. The most obvious recent example is President Trump's redirection of military funds to building border fencing. There have been less controversial engagements as well. In 2010, with high numbers of illegal crossings in Arizona, President Obama deployed 1,200 National Guard troops to the border to assist with surveillance to identify illicit crossings and analyze intelligence. Additionally, in 2014 when the flows of unaccompanied children from Central America overwhelmed the shelter capacity of the Health and Human Services, empty space on military bases was used to provide temporary housing while the migrants were processed. Generally, these efforts have been reluctant and Defense resists having any significant role in homeland security efforts.

Defense is organized toward international offensive operations, and already generally has forward deployed troops and authorities and processes in place to deploy special forces, so it is a much more direct and simple shift for them to conduct international operations to kill terrorists than to deal with domestic vulnerabilities. This is exemplified by the operations of the Joint Special Operations Command, which were authorized by Secretary Donald Rumsfeld in 2003 with an order authorizing military action against terrorists anywhere in the world without prior congressional or presidential approval.[16]

After 9/11 Defense established a new Northern Command (universally referred to as NORTHCOM) that oversees domestic activities in addition to Canada and Mexico. There is also an assistant secretary for homeland defense and counternarcotics, although people in this position are careful to define their role as focused on threats that originate outside of the homeland. This is the reason that the international Ebola response described in the introduction, which was led by Defense and well resourced, was so much more decisive and clear than the muddled response to domestic infections. They do this in part because of the stringent restrictions on the military role in domestic law enforcement activities put in place with the post–Civil War Posse Comitatus Act, although this does not limit significant preparedness and response work that is not directly law enforcement. Additionally, as will be discussed in more detail later, Defense has enormous influence over the U.S. government's cybersecurity efforts, with the result that these efforts continue to be focused internationally and on offensive operations rather than on the protection of critical domestic systems.

4 | The Department of Homeland Security We Have

The previous chapter focused on the process of change since 2001, and this chapter will provide a deeper description of DHS as it currently exists and some tools to evaluate its policies and decisions. In the process of shifting to deal with national security threats with much broader domestic implications, this will help demonstrate what we have got right about the shift and the questions that remain unaddressed.

There is a central disconnect between DHS's mission and its activities. Fundamentally, DHS was created to make sure that the 9/11 attacks are never repeated, which means ensuring that trained terrorist operatives are never again able to enter the United States and perpetrate a mass casualty attack. The 9/11 attack is the essential part of the public and internal understanding of the DHS mission. As an example, the commissioner of CBP has a wall-sized image of Ground Zero in Manhattan next to his desk, looming over all of the work done in the office. This understanding and sense of responsibility is the single most important factor unifying a department that has many elements with missions that are otherwise extremely disparate.

However, most of the work that DHS does day to day doesn't actually deal with countering terrorism, and much of the counterterrorism work done by the U.S. government is not part of the department—it is done by the Intelligence Community and the Departments of Justice and Defense. As shown in the discussion of Ebola in the introduction, DHS is also not in a position to lead civilian safety efforts across government, and coordinates with Health and Human Services and CDC on emergency medical response. DHS, because of the decisions that were made when it was formed, has broad responsibilities that focus in a few key areas. The department's primary work has to do with securing critical systems of commerce and travel, and preparing for and responding to disasters.

The following section describes what DHS actually does, and will likely be basic to those who are already familiar with the department. I have included it because of the frequent broad misconceptions about the role of DHS or its components, even among people who work regularly with DHS.

The Operational Components of DHS

The DHS organizational chart is a daunting graphic, with 30+ different boxes with hierarchies and lines of authority unclear. Each of these boxes can then be Russian nesting dolls of additional structures and hierarchies. For example, the commissioner of CBP, represented by a single box on the organizational chart, oversees over 60,000 people, with a deputy commissioner, six executive assistant commissioners including the chief of the Border Patrol, and 10 assistant commissioners. On the other hand, the assistant secretary for public affairs, which represents another box on the DHS organizational chart, has an entire staff of under 20. The result of the lopsided division of responsibilities is that overviews or summaries of the department can obscure where the largest functions of the organization and budget actually reside.

To understand DHS, it is most helpful to think in terms of the operational components that execute its missions. There are (only) eight of these, and they take up the vast majority of attention from managers. If you can keep track of these eight, and a few of the key organizations within them listed below, you will have a pretty good understanding of what the department is doing. Most of the other entities either provide support to these operational components or coordinate policy or outreach related to their activities. The components are listed below along with their staff, primary responsibilities, and budget.* Within these operational components, a few key subcomponents are described in additional detail.

- Transportation Security Administration (TSA)
  - TSA is perhaps the most visible part of Homeland Security and has over 50,000 employees who inspect everyone getting on a plane in the United States. This component also includes air

---

* All budget figures are taken from https://www.dhs.gov/sites/default/files/publications/19_0318_MGMT_FY-2020-Budget-In-Brief.pdf

marshals who ride undercover and armed on commercial flights, and a significant international presence that works to ensure that last point of departure airports (foreign locations with direct flights to the United States) meet appropriate security standards. The Secure Flight program, which will be discussed in more detail in the section on targeting, is the main mechanism by which domestic passengers are vetted against watch lists before they board a plane.

- Annual Budget (2018): $7,841,355,000
- *What the Transportation Security Administration does:*
  Screens passengers boarding domestic and international flights.
  Runs the Secure Flight vetting program to identify high-risk travelers.
  Ensures security standards are met at airports where planes depart for the United States.
  Puts armed air marshals on flights in case of attempted hijackings and other threats.
  Works with public and private stakeholders on all surface transportation systems, such as highways and commuter rail systems.
- *What the Transportation Security Administration does not do:*
  While its name implies responsibility for all modes of transportation for both people and freight, and roads, trains, and subways are technically included in its mission, very little of the component's attention goes to anything other than aviation security. Their employees are rarely involved in security at any other transportation mode (even something as high profile as the Washington, DC, metro is generally secured by local police).
- Customs and Border Protection (CBP)†
  - This is America's border management agency. It includes about 21,000 green-uniformed Border Patrol agents who patrol the borders and stop illicit crossings; 23,000 blue-uniformed CBP officers who process goods and people at the 328 ports of entry

---

† Please, please, do not call it "Customs and Border Patrol." This drives the two-thirds of the agency that do not work in the Border Patrol crazy and is a sloppy mistake that constantly finds its way into news articles and public statements.

to the United States; and an Air and Marine office with planes, helicopters, and boats that surveils and interdicts illegal traffic (there is some overlap with this mission and that of the Coast Guard). The National Targeting Center is the primary means by which international travelers and cargo bound for the United States are assessed by risk.

- Annual Budget (2018): $16,315,216,000
- *What CBP does:*
  Prevents illegal border crossing and interdicts illegal migrants and smugglers.
  Processes passengers and goods at all U.S. legal border crossing locations and at 14 preclearance locations around the world and identifies and seizes contraband.
  Vets all travelers entering the United States against watch lists and targeting rules.
  Runs extensive air and marine operations to interdict illegal crossing between the ports of entry.
  Inspects agricultural goods to identify and stop plant pests.
  Enforces customs and intellectual property rights rules and collects revenue on dutiable goods.
- *What CBP does not do:*
  Any investigations other than internal affairs.
  CBP is legally required not to detain migrants for longer than 72 hours; once migrants go through Border Patrol in-processing they are required to be moved to another agency within three days. Adults are generally referred to ICE and children sent to Health and Human Services. When processing backups have occurred, most significantly after the Trump administration's implementation of a "zero tolerance" policy that referred adults for prosecution while separating them from their children, overcrowding at Border Patrol processing centers led to the widely publicized images of children crowded behind chain link fences.
- Immigration and Customs Enforcement (ICE)
  - Immigration and Customs Enforcement, or ICE as it is generally known, consists of nearly 20,000 full-time employees, with the majority being either investigators in Homeland Security Investigations or the officers involved in detention and removal of

immigration violators. Because federal legal authorities at the border are extremely broad, ICE has a wider mandate than other federal investigative agencies, such as the Federal Bureau of Investigation or the Drug Enforcement Administration. ICE investigates immigration violations, customs, terrorism, human smuggling and trafficking, narcotics, intellectual property violations, artifact and art smuggling, and more. ICE also contains the office of Enforcement and Removal Operations, which is responsible for detaining and removing illegal migrants. This requires a significant amount of coordination with state and local law enforcement, who may encounter criminals who are in the United States illegally, and with foreign governments, who must supply travel documents before anyone can be removed. Enforcement and Removal Operations also has fugitive operations teams that work to track down criminals and others who have been ordered removed. This is consistently the most controversial part of DHS, and objections to removals have led to calls to "abolish" the component entirely. These topics will be addressed in more detail in chapter 8, which focuses on migration.

- Annual Budget (2018): $7,452,484,000
- *What ICE does:*

  Investigates immigration and customs violations, as well as transnational organized crime, human trafficking and smuggling, intellectual property rights violations, narcotics, art and artifact smuggling, and more.

  Detains and removes immigration violators and criminal aliens.

  Operates in 46 countries to investigate immigration and customs violations in partnership with local authorities.

  ICE attorneys represent the U.S. government in immigration court proceedings.
- *What ICE does not do:*

  ICE does not investigate drugs smuggled between the ports of entry and smugglers apprehended by Border Patrol, which are handled by the Drug Enforcement Administration.

  ICE does not detain unaccompanied children, and, because of a court order, cannot currently detain families for more than 21 days.

  ICE is not the lead U.S. investigative agency for counterterrorism.

ICE cannot remove people without valid travel documents, which requires coordination with home country embassies or consulates.

- Citizenship and Immigration Services (CIS)
  - Citizenship and Immigration Services, or CIS, is the agency that grants or denies immigration benefits. It consists of 17,000 staff with about 230 domestic and foreign offices, and they determine eligibility to enter and stay in the United States through review of cases and interviews. They have a fraud detection and national security division that is responsible for investigating things like marriage fraud and identifying national security threats among the people who have already received visas and are legitimately eligible to enter the United States.
  - Annual Budget (2018): $4,482,039,000
  - *What Citizenship and Immigration Services does:*
    Processes applications for immigration benefits, such as green cards.
    Naturalizes new citizens.
    Investigates immigration fraud.
    Manages the E-Verify program that allows companies to check work eligibility.
    Interviews and screens potential refugees and manages the asylum application process. On the Southwest border, this means making an initial determination about whether an individual's asylum claims meet a "credible fear" standard that prevents them from being quickly removed.
  - *What Citizenship and Immigration Services does not do:*
    CIS is not a law enforcement agency and does not take any law enforcement actions for immigration violations.
    CIS does not actually give individual visas, which is done by the State Department.
- Coast Guard
  - The Coast Guard is both part of DHS and a military service, and as such is comparatively independent of the department's oversight. The Coast Guard is responsible for securing U.S. ports, inland waterways, coasts, and the zone in which the United States has exclusive jurisdiction around its coasts.
  - Annual Budget (2018): $12,265,631,000

- *What the Coast Guard does:*
  Responds to maritime threats and disasters.
  Rescues people in distress at sea.
  Patrols the coastal regions, inland waterways, and ports, and
    boards and intercepts high-interest vessels that could be smug-
    gling people or contraband.
  Regulates hazardous cargo and ensures that parties responsi-
    ble for environmental damage to waterways are held
    accountable.
  Maritime law enforcement including arresting contraband
    smugglers.
- *What the Coast Guard does not do:*
  The Coast Guard actually is not the exclusive entity within DHS
    for maritime interdiction. CBP's Air and Marine branch also
    maintains a large fleet of ships and planes and does a large
    amount of intercepting dangerous vessels. In the Caribbean,
    drug and migrant interdiction responsibilities are divided by
    an interagency center called the Joint Interagency Task Force—
    South (or JIATF-S, pronounced jee-aaah-tiff S).
- Secret Service
  - The Secret Service is made up of about 6,700 employees with the
    primary responsibility of dignitary protection, most visibly for
    the first family. The Secret Service handles the security for for-
    eign heads of state, and major events like the UN General
    Assembly in New York or other large international conferences
    that are held in Washington, DC (the African Leaders Summit
    conference in 2014 is a major example and involved the heads of
    state from 50 different countries).
  - Annual Budget (2018): $2,271,524,000
  - *What the Secret Service does:*
    Protects the life of the president and first family, former presi-
      dents and their spouses, presidential and vice-presidential
      candidates, cabinet members, and foreign heads of state.
    Investigates threats against protectees.
    Investigates counterfeiting and other financial and cyber crimes.
  - *What the Secret Service does not do:*
    Protect members of Congress, who are protected by the Capitol
      Police.

- Federal Emergency Management Agency (FEMA)
  - FEMA, as it is universally known, handles disasters and coordinates the federal response, works with affected states and communities, and directly provides resources to ensure preparation for and recovery from disasters. Whereas most of the rest of DHS tries to stop bad things from happening, FEMA focuses on what to do if something bad does occur. It is one of the most independent of the DHS components, as it was previously an independent agency and the administrator has effective cabinet status during emergencies, and has about 9,000 employees.
  - Annual Budget (2018): $17,332,468,000
  - *What FEMA does:*
    Works with state, local, and tribal entities to prepare for, protect against, respond to, recover from, and mitigate any kinds of hazards.
    Provides grants to local communities and cities to improve preparedness.
    Manages the coordinated federal response to disasters.
    Provides direct funding to communities and people who are victims of disasters through the Disaster Relief Fund.
    Subsidizes flood insurance through the National Flood Insurance Program.
  - *What FEMA does not do:*
    FEMA is not a law enforcement agency and does not handle maintaining order and preventing activities like looting after natural disasters.
    FEMA is not a primary response agency; it does not generally provide resources directly but instead coordinates emergency response among other federal, state, and local entities.
- Cybersecurity and Infrastructure Security Agency (CISA)
  - This component is responsible for DHS's cybersecurity work and protecting federal buildings, in addition to policy responsibilities related to critical infrastructure and container security. DHS is the U.S. government's lead for civilian cybersecurity, and executes those responsibilities through this component, which has about 3,500 employees.
  - Annual Budget (2018): $3,387,457,000

- *What CISA does:*

  Partners with the private sector and other members of the community on civilian cybersecurity to strengthen protections in privately owned systems and to quickly identify and address breaches.

  Oversees the Federal Protective Service, the entity that protects federal buildings and facilities.

  Protects critical infrastructure by working with private and non-federal infrastructure owners to build response capabilities and sharing information about risks.

- *What CISA does not do:*

  Cyber warfare and cyber defense, which are done by other federal agencies.

  CISA used to work with the Department of Energy and the Intelligence Community to prevent the proliferation of nuclear materials, but in December 2017 this function was moved to a new DHS Countering Weapons of Mass Destruction Office.

Management Challenges in DHS

Unsurprisingly, this sprawling structure and these diverse missions generate management problems. The sheer size of the organization and the dramatic variation between the component missions creates enormous challenges for department leadership. DHS is the third largest department in the government, after Defense and Veterans Affairs, with over 240,000 employees. In addition to the operational offices listed above, there are headquarters offices responsible for policy, outreach to Congress, intergovernmental relations, intelligence and analysis, private sector outreach, management and budget, legal issues, and operations coordination. Many of these offices are replicated within the individual components, which inevitably results in parallel staff with different priorities. Congressional affairs staffers from components as different as CIS and the Secret Service will never independently arrive at the same priorities, and the headquarters congressional team has little direct authority over them. Effectively, the only two officials that everyone in the department recognizes that they report to are the secretary and the deputy secretary. By any reasonable standard it is clear that the secretary of DHS has too many direct reports to actively manage. This results in far too many decisions that should have been resolved at a lower level being pushed up to the department leadership. It also means that it is often difficult for leadership to oversee and control the actions of components absent direct engagement from the secretary's office, which reduces the effectiveness of the other headquarters offices charged with coordination across the components.

Additionally, because of the large number of issues that are managed and decided through the White House NSC Principals Committee and Deputies Committee meetings, the secretary and deputy secretary have constant obligations to attend meetings at the White House. Deputy secretaries or their designees will sometimes have to attend multiple meetings a day in the Situation Room, which requires a great deal of preparation and back and forth travel and can leave little time to actually focus on running the department. This is particularly onerous for DHS officials because the headquarters is quite a bit farther away from the White House than most other departments. Combined with the enormous amount of time required to prepare for congressional hearings and respond to other forms of congressional oversight and the necessary meetings with key stakeholders who are interested in DHS operations, executives can very easily find all of their time taken up by activities that are unrelated to their management and policy priorities.

Morale is bad at DHS although it varies considerably across different parts of the organization. The department has consistently fared poorly in employee satisfaction surveys, with results that have been among the lowest or the lowest in government.[1] Fixing the issue of employee morale will take a sustained and well-resourced effort over the course of years if not decades. The low morale is generally driven by three factors. The first is that some of the missions are just unpleasant. Nobody particularly likes having to arrest and deport children and families, or having to pat down hundreds of irritated air travelers. Certain components like ICE's Enforcement and Removal Operations or TSA screeners will just never compete with agencies like NASA on employee morale. Second, the employees without a clear sense of mission or who feel like they are doing something other than their real mission will be unhappy. A recent example is the Border Patrol as they have responded to the influx of Central American children. Border Patrol recruiting efforts emphasize military-like activities and show agents riding all terrain vehicles and riding horses. The Border Patrol agents this attracts want to be out in the field stopping and arresting potentially dangerous people, not sitting in the sector headquarters distributing diapers and food. And third, components that have significant management problems and public failures are particularly susceptible to having dispirited employees. Morale in the Secret Service plummeted after a series of management shakeups were precipitated by a White House fence jumper who managed to enter the bottom floor of the residence before being captured. TSA also had most of its management replaced after a "red team" exercise, in which undercover agents attempted to bring contraband through airport checkpoints, showed that their officers failed 67 of the 70 tests conducted.[2]

DHS also has personnel management problems stemming from the circumstances of its establishment. When it was created, many individuals from related agencies took advantage of the opportunity to move to the new agency and be promoted into higher ranking positions, often motivated by the desire for a promotion rather than an interest in the mission. As a result, there are components with completely disproportionate numbers of nonsupervisory senior officials—people getting paid close to $200,000 a year who produce work at nowhere near the level of competence that would be expected. It's also important to understand that there was no bench for DHS political appointees. Consecutive two-term presidents from different parties for the first thirteen years of the department meant that nobody in a political appointment had served in a previous administration until 2017. This had predictable effects on the consistency and quality of the department's management.

There are a number of different models that have been tried to manage the department to date, and they have various strengths and weaknesses that correspond to the extent to which control is centralized in the secretary's office. The most common has been to establish a group of trusted "counselors" (the exact titles have varied under different secretaries) who have specific policy portfolios that run across different parts of DHS and are able to speak for the secretary when working with the leadership of the different components. As an example a counselor could be responsible for counterterrorism and countering violent extremism, while another could do maritime and aviation security, while another does border security. This has the benefit of centralizing the decision-making and providing a predictable point of contact to the component executives for specified issues. Generally these roles are filled by political appointees, who do not have to go through the lengthy hiring process that exists for career staffers. This gives secretaries the ability to quickly put in place a small team of people they have worked with and trust. It can result, however, in a disconnect between the secretary's staff and the component leadership, as the key staff are all located in headquarters and have little direct experience with the different components. Because the staff in the secretary's office will always be most focused on issues confronting the secretary and interagency coordination issues and especially deliverables for the White House, they may not be able to identify and resolve emergent issues from the components as quickly and responsively as necessary.

The details of how the secretary's office is organized have varied, but in my experience the keys are to have a limited number of extremely capable people working very hard who have clear portfolios and defined access to the secretary, who can be the primary points of contact for specific issues and provide guidance and feedback. It is essential that the secretary's staff, wherever they are located, see themselves as a two-way conduit for information, as opposed to just the mechanism by which tasks are communicated down to the components. The staffers who are most successful in these roles are the ones who make an attempt to actually help the leadership of the components and to keep them from being surprised by things coming from the secretary's office, to the extent that is possible. If the career executives from across the agency are unclear about who speaks for the secretary on which issues or what the priorities and direction really are, confusion and inefficiency very quickly follow.

Because the department is so sprawling, the requirements on the leadership are so varied, and the bureaucracy is comparatively immature, senior officials who begin work at the department can quickly find themselves in situations for which they are alarmingly unprepared. When this occurs in meetings with foreign leaders or with counterparts at the White House, the reaction of their staffs is generally to put new, more rigorous requirements in place. These normally manifest themselves in terms of materials needing to be prepared days or weeks in advance of meetings, preparatory briefings, and stringent new requirements for the background information that has to be included (executives invariably have slightly different preferences on how the information should be presented). These efforts are well intentioned, but quickly just add new layers to the bureaucratic confusion that already exists and generally have the opposite of the intended effect. The only way for a senior official to be well prepared at DHS is to have a small group of key staffers who are working extremely hard who interact with the bureaucracy, provide constant guidance and feedback, and are able to ensure that the necessary information is in front of the executive at the right time.

Other departments have much more mature structures in place to support their leadership. In the Department of State, for example, senior foreign service officers will do tours in the department's Executive Secretariat, or work as confidential assistants to Senate confirmed appointees. This is not the case at DHS. The Executive Secretariat is staffed with some very good people, but they have essentially no authority over the people who have to provide them with materials, and they quickly become beleaguered and harried by the competing demands of and constant interactions with angry senior staffers. Additionally, the kind of people who join the State Department are generally people who don't mind writing reports or memos, whereas at DHS the staffer who is tasked with writing briefing materials could be a Border Patrol agent who was forced to do a shift at headquarters and never wanted to even spend their days in a building, let alone writing talking points.

As a staffer it could be incredibly frustrating trying to navigate incoherent and contradictory requirements while creating preparatory materials. This could also sometimes be amusing, if you were able to take a step back. I was working in DHS International Affairs when our office, somehow, was tasked with writing a briefing memorandum and read-ahead materials for the secretary to attend a presidential speech to a joint session of Congress. The Executive Secretariat refused to accept our materials without the required talking points, and was not interested in hearing us explain that the secretary would not, and really should not, be doing any speaking at this event. One of my colleagues was so frustrated he began typing out a sheet of talking points along these lines:

- [clap clap clap clap clap]
- [*nodding thoughtfully*]
- [clap clap clap clap clap clap clap]
- [*remains awake*]
- [*standing:* clap clap clap clap clap clap clap]

Eventually we were able to get ahold of someone in the front office who confirmed that the secretary didn't need talking points for an event at which she was not speaking.

DHS Oversight

DHS also has extremely convoluted and unproductive congressional oversight. One of the basic facts of life in Washington, DC, is that once a congressional committee is given oversight over part of the executive branch, it will never willingly give that oversight up. As a result, when DHS was created it retained nearly all of the oversight authorities that existed from legacy organizations and then added a number of new layers focused on the new department specifically. The result is that the DHS answers to some 119 congressional committees and subcommittees,[3] with a continuous schedule of hearings, reports, and demands for information. This is, at best, extremely distracting from the work of actual management and mission execution. The result is that backlogs of materials mean Congress doesn't get the timely information it needs while DHS officials are constantly overwhelmed.

The two things that congressional overseers are best at rooting out are incompetence and inappropriate political influence (by the other party), and they look very, very hard for these. Civil servants are used to a level of scrutiny that people who have mostly worked in the private sector can find intolerable; the business equivalent would be like being in the middle of multiple extremely contentious lawsuits all the time with unpredictable parties who all have huge resources. This experience is particularly exaggerated at DHS, especially in politically sensitive places like ICE or the Border Patrol, where new staffers need to approach their jobs with the expectation that every email they send or document they touch could and probably will be made public in as unflattering a context as possible.

This is very difficult to balance because people at DHS complain accurately that there is too much overlapping oversight, but then inevitably there are scandals and the response is that everyone demands more oversight. Identifying incompetence and preventing inappropriate political influence are important, but in a time like this when government is transitioning to deal with new threats the oversight should be more focused on the issue of balance as resources shift and regulations change. A new department will inevitably involve a certain amount of waste and duplication, which needs to be stopped, but there are major questions that overseers must help address about how DHS balances individual rights and privacy against collective security. It is absolutely essential that overseers focus on creating effective systems for redress and to challenge abuses and oversteps, and not just to find and punish incompetence.

The DHS International Presence and Role

Despite the tension it causes with other agencies the DHS international role is continuing to grow. This can be expected to continue as homeland security considerations increasingly need to be integrated into foreign policy planning. DHS needs to improve its organization for international engagements and manage the process of asserting its interests without creating unnecessary conflict with the State Department (some conflict is inevitable). DHS has an extremely large but fragmented international presence, the third largest for any civilian department in the U.S. government. ICE, CBP, the Coast Guard, and TSA each have large international deployments and constant engagement with foreign counterparts. The difficult work of establishing mechanisms to coordinate across the department's international affairs function and exercising direct control over the international presence of components is in a fairly early stage compared to more established departments.

Under the guidance of Assistant Secretary for Policy Alan Bersin, who was also designated the department's chief diplomatic officer in 2012, the department took steps to organize and expand its international engagement and to ensure a unified approach through the development of regional strategies. One of the most urgent needs within DHS is for an integrated international presence with a clear career path for its international officers. This should include language training, opportunities for experience at multiple embassies, understanding other U.S. entities operating internationally, and training across DHS components. The substantive work that is done on homeland security issues offers high-level engagement with foreign officials on important and interesting issues, and should appeal to the kinds of people who are attracted to careers in foreign relations. Unfortunately, what often happens is that international jobs are used as another avenue for promotion for people who wouldn't be promoted within their existing operational channel, rather than the true career path that they should be.

Working with international partners, especially in terms of training and capacity building, requires a great deal of coordination within the U.S. government. Law enforcement agencies like DHS (along with the Department of Justice) cannot directly provide foreign aid. This must be done through coordination with the Department of State's International Narcotics and Law Enforcement division, which funds training conducted by other departments. This creates bureaucratic layers on top of bureaucratic layers when key policy decisions have already been made, and ensures that if there are personality conflicts between, say, a DHS attaché and the State Department Bureau of International Narcotics and Law Enforcement country director, training and capacity building programs will be significantly affected. The process of using foreign aid for law enforcement missions needs a senior level review, as there may be significant benefits to letting law enforcement agencies run and pay for their own training and capacity building efforts.

| DHS has a particularly expansive role within North America. Canada and Mexico are consistently among the United States' three largest trading partners, along with China. This actually understates their economic importance to the United States, however, because our trade with them is much more balanced between imports and exports than trade with Asia, where the vast majority of goods are imported to the United States. The United States and Canada are as closely interconnected culturally and economically as any two countries in the world. There are 40 million citizens of Mexican descent now living in the United States, which now has roughly as many native Spanish speakers as Spain does.[4]

North America's populations are extraordinarily interconnected and local officials interact daily and productively, but the U.S. government as a whole is inadequately focused on North America. Inherently transnational twenty-first-century threats mean the security importance of Canada and Mexico is vastly increased. Much, much more attention should be directed at the senior level to cooperation with Canada and Mexico on a wide range of issues, but especially cooperation on issues related to homeland security.

A former Mexican ambassador to the United States once explained that part of his job was to go around Washington, DC, reminding everyone that "Mexico is not Croatia." It was a joke but is also a useful reminder that our relationship with Mexico is simply not comparable to other foreign relations. The law professor Bayless Manning first used a term that neatly (if inelegantly) summarizes the relationship as "intermestic," that is, not international and not domestic but featuring intermingled aspects of the two. This clashes with the traditional orientation of foreign policy, however, which is that all foreign interactions should be channeled through the State Department. Institutionally the U.S. government is not focused on this engagement—the highest-ranking official responsible specifically for Mexico at the State Department headquarters is an office director. This extends across government: the NSC recently had multiple directors for Syria but only one director responsible for both Mexico and Canada. Part of the problem is that the U.S. government at the federal level has been oriented to treat interactions with Canada and Mexico as foreign relations issues, rather than the intermestic interactions that take place daily. Additionally, there is an institutional bias because the types of people who join the State Department generally are not hoping to spend years becoming Canada specialists and mastering the intricacies of bureaucratic maneuvering in a country culturally similar to the United States.

Part of this engagement gap has been filled by DHS. The department has more day to day interaction with Canadian and Mexican officials and citizens than any other department by a significant margin. The secretary is the primary counterpart for both Mexico's secretary of finance, who oversees customs functions, and Mexico's secretary of the interior, traditionally the second most powerful figure in the Mexican government, overseeing migration and security. In Canada, the key counterpart is the minister of public safety and emergency preparedness, who oversees not only the Canadian Border Services Agency but also the Royal Canadian Mounted Police (the main federal police force, with responsibilities that in the United States would encompass the FBI, the Drug Enforcement Administration (DEA), ICE, the Bureau of Alcohol, Tobacco, Firearms and Explosives, and the Border Patrol) and the Canadian Secret Intelligence Service, their central intelligence agency. DHS officials, therefore, spend a disproportionate amount of time interacting with Canadian and Mexican counterparts and have developed effective bilateral mechanisms.

This is clearly a good thing. The United States should be more, not less, engaged with Canada and Mexico. Bureaucratic turf wrangling should not obscure the very significant benefits of close DHS interaction with North American counterparts. For every instance in which a lack of coordination between DHS and State creates problems, there are dozens of instances where the fact of close collaboration between U.S. and Mexican officials is of enormous benefit to the people of both countries. The expansion of the bilateral relationship should not be held back because government agencies want to protect their fiefdoms.

The lack of trilateral North American institutions is striking, and should be remedied. The "Five Eyes," made up of the United States, Canada, New Zealand, Australia, and the United Kingdom, have extensive and intricate networks of coordination for security issues. There are special categories of intelligence to allow sharing between them, there are annual meetings between the heads of customs, the heads of intelligence, the interior ministers, the defense ministers, the heads of immigration, and the attorneys general. North America, on the other hand, has only trilateral defense and foreign ministerial meetings.

Evaluating Homeland Security Policy Questions

The activities of the department are so varied and technical that important policy issues can seem daunting for anyone not immersed in the details of an issue. There are, however, a few guidelines that can help organize the major issues that could come up. Homeland security policy questions require a different framework than traditional military or foreign policy questions.

Checklists can help organize our thoughts when we deal with complicated questions, and when dealing with policy issues they can improve the quality of analysis and enable better decision-making. Below is a short checklist of considerations for any homeland security initiative or policy change. This list is based on my experience dealing with policy questions at the DHS and the NSC.

1. Who are the major stakeholders in this decision, and who would stand to gain and to lose? This should include government entities, state and local communities, the private sector, and any international interests.
2. Does this cost money?[‡] If so, who will pay for it? If it is going to

---

‡ Considerations of cost should always include the staff time, which, especially for law enforcement officers, is expensive and in demand.

be the federal government, will it come from appropriated funds? If so, will it be from existing appropriations or will it require new money from Congress? If it is going to be paid by a fee, who will pay the fee? Are those who will pay the fee willing to do so or will they complain?

3. How will Congress react? Are there any legislative changes required, both in the United States or in foreign countries, or both? Are there legislative backers for this? How long will it take for the legislation to be entered into law?

4. How long will this last? If it is ongoing, is it self-sustaining? If it is not ongoing, is there a specific end date? If not, how will that be decided?

5. Are there any legal, privacy, or environmental issues? How will those be addressed?

6. Is there data that can inform this decision? Are there other inputs that should have been considered?

7. Who will implement this, and who will oversee implementation? Does this align with the mission of the institution, or is there another entity that would be better placed to do this? What are the opportunity costs?

8. How will the implementation of this initiative or change be measured? What will the metrics be? Are appropriate data collections mechanisms in place to track this and determine success or failure?

9. What other alternatives were considered? Are there any others that should have been considered that were not?

10. Have all of the possible secondary outcomes or unintended consequences been thought through?

11. Is there a strong political reason for this initiative?

By running through these questions you can evaluate proposals in a structured way, identify likely problems in advance, and help prevent surprises when things don't turn out as expected.

As an example of how this would work in practice, I'll use this process to evaluate the 2010 deployment of 1,200 National Guard troops to the Southwest border to assist in border security efforts. I'll approach the initiative as if I were a policy analyst in 2010 looking at it as a proposal before it had been implemented.

1. Who are the major stakeholders in this decision, and who would stand to gain and to lose? This should include government entities, state and local communities, the private sector, and any international interests.

The major federal stakeholders are Defense and DHS. The NSC and the Domestic Policy Council at the White House will also be deeply interested. The governors of the four border states will want advance notice and have strong responses, as will mayors and community leaders from cities along the border. Advocacy groups will be concerned about using troops at the border for a law enforcement function. The government of Mexico will likely be concerned about the treatment of migrants and the perception of militarizing the border.

2. Does this cost money? If so, who will pay for it? If it is going to be the federal government, will it come from appropriated funds? If so, will it come from existing appropriations or will it require new money from Congress? If it is going to be paid by a fee, who will pay the fee? Are those who will pay the fee willing to do so or will they complain?

This does cost money, and it will be paid for jointly by Defense and DHS. It will use existing appropriated funds. Defense will likely resist paying for this.

3. How will Congress react? Are there any legislative changes required, both in the United States or in foreign countries, or both? Are there legislative backers for this? How long will it take for the legislation to be entered into law?

This does not require legislation, but Congress will be intensely interested. Many Democrats will oppose this as militarizing the border, and Republicans will attack it as inadequate.

4. How long will this last? If it is ongoing, is it self-sustaining? If it is not ongoing, is there a specific end date? If not, how will that be decided?

It's currently a one-year deployment, although it is not clear whether it will be extended. The secretaries of DHS and Defense will have to decide whether this should be continued in coordination with the White House.

5. Are there any legal, privacy, or environmental issues? How will those be addressed?

There are legal issues around what the National Guard troops can and can't do while assisting law enforcement, which will restrict their activities. There are not any obvious privacy or environmental issues.

6. Is there data that can inform this decision? Are there other inputs that should have been considered?

The most relevant metric is the number of apprehensions made by the Border Patrol along the Southwest border. Apprehensions have been declining up to 2010, which would indicate that this might not be necessary, although they have increased in Arizona's Tucson Sector.

7. Who will implement this, and who will oversee implementation? Does this align with the mission of the institution, or is there another entity that would be better placed to do this? What are the opportunity costs?

This will be implemented by the National Guard and overseen by their chain of command, although as they will be assisting the Border Patrol on its mission they will be responding to requests from the Border Patrol and DHS leadership. This mostly aligns with the National Guard's mission if you see the situation at the border as a national emergency. This was probably more true of the situation in 2000 than the situation in 2010. There are about 18,000 Border Patrol agents on the Southwest border working on this mission, and they can do this more effectively because they can actually arrest immigration violators. This will take National Guard members away from other important duties.

8. How will the implementation of this initiative or change be measured? What will the metrics be? Are appropriate data col-

lection mechanisms in place to track this and determine success or failure?

This is tricky, because it could both help the Border Patrol to apprehend more people and deter more crossings with a heavier presence at the border. Thus, if apprehensions go either up or down it could be argued that this is successful, or not. The specific hours of surveillance assistance provided by the National Guard could also be tracked, although this is just an input and not an indicator of whether the initiative is successful.

9. What other alternatives were considered? Are there any others that should have been considered that were not?

The alternatives would include redeploying more Border Patrol agents from other parts of the country, such as the northern border. The administration could also ask Congress through the president's budget for an increase in Border Patrol staffing or funding for additional flight hours from the Air and Marine branch that supports them. An alternative that could have been considered would be to provide direct assistance to Mexican federal law enforcement authorities, enabling them to do more migration enforcement on their side of the border. This could have potentially provided more benefit in terms of reduced crossings and smuggling for the money spent.

10. Have all of the possible secondary outcomes or unintended consequences been thought through?

This could drive migrants to more remote parts of the border and make crossing more dangerous. It could also increase the costs for coyotes (guides), which would result in greater revenue for criminal organizations.

11. Is there a strong political reason for this initiative?

Yes, the Obama administration wants to advance comprehensive immigration reform and needs to be seen as taking strong border security steps in order to make that happen.

Running through this checklist makes it easier to think through all the implications of the initiative in a more organized and thorough way than just trying to decide "do I think it's a good idea or not to send the National Guard to the border now," and to make sure there aren't any important considerations that have been missed. Having gone through the checklist with the National Guard deployment from the perspective of an analyst, I would have concluded that it was not necessarily merited operationally but probably made sense in the political context.

❚ This book isn't focused on my disagreements with the Trump administration but it seems negligent to not discuss the two most high-profile initial homeland security proposals by the administration: the plan to build a wall across the entire southern border and be reimbursed by the Mexican government, and the executive order stopping all travel from Iran, Iraq, Syria, Yemen, Sudan, Somalia, and Libya, along with a suspension of the refugee admission program for 120 days. President Trump's proposals are deeply twentieth-century, nation-state-centered responses to a perceived threat. I used this checklist to analyze both issues in early 2017 shortly after the executive order on the travel ban was announced, and rather than update them to reflect newer information, I will leave them as they were as an example of trying to evaluate homeland security policy questions in real time and let readers judge how well they have held up.

Building a Wall along the Border That Mexico Will Pay For

1. Who are the major stakeholders in this decision, and who would stand to gain and to lose? This should include government entities, state and local communities, the private sector, and any international interests.

U.S. and Mexican companies that move goods across the border, intending migrants from Mexico and other countries, Mexican officials who are dealing with U.S. counterparts, American companies and individuals who hire migrants, Mexican elected officials who would have to approve a reimbursement for the wall, border communities, tribes adjacent to the border, and private landowners on whose property the wall would be built.

2. Does this cost money? If so, who will pay for it? If it is going to be the federal government, will it come from appropriated funds? If so, will it come from existing appropriations or will it require new money from Congress? If it is going to be paid by a fee, who will pay the fee? Are those who will pay the fee willing to do so or will they complain?

The latest credible estimates are over $20 billion, and from my own experience I imagine this estimate is for a scaled-down version and that sum significantly understates the cost of the kind of wall that President Trump described in public statements. I have seen CBP estimates of the cost of simply removing the cane fields that cover much of the border around the Rio Grande Valley and in which migrants can hide that would cost close to $7 billion. Requirements that a wall be made with American produced steel will increase the cost further. There is no appropriated funding for this. The Mexican government could only possibly be made to pay for the wall through some kind of extreme coercion; no Mexican elected official would be able to stay in office after supporting Mexican payment for this wall. Even if the U.S. government were to somehow force the existing Mexican administration to pay for the construction it would never be approved by the Mexican Congress and it would guarantee a party change in the 2018 presidential elections to someone much more hostile to U.S. interests.

3. How will Congress react? Are there any legislative changes required, both in the U.S. or in foreign countries, or both? Are there legislative backers for this? How long will it take for the legislation to be entered into law?

Republicans in Congress are generally supportive of this, although the extent to which they are willing to appropriate billions of dollars for this construction is very much in question. The administration is currently developing their proposal for the 2018 budget (federal budgeting is a cumbersome and delay-filled process), so absent some pretty creative budgeting the earliest these funds would begin to be made available would be sometime in 2018.[5]

4. How long will this last? If it is ongoing, is it self-sustaining? If it is not ongoing, is there a specific end date? If not, how will that be decided?

There would not be an end date for the wall; the construction would be expected to be permanent. There would be enormous upkeep costs for this kind of facility that would require a major expansion in the CBP facilities management budget.

5. Are there any legal, privacy, or environmental issues? How will those be addressed?

There are major legal issues around the land that is not owned by the federal government, which includes much of the space adjacent to the border in Texas as well as the sovereign territory of Indian tribes, most significantly the Tohono O'odham Nation that covers 72 miles of the Arizona/Sonora border. In many locations building a wall would require large-scale condemnation of private land through eminent domain. There will also be major environmental issues. The existing fencing required waivers of environmental regulations for construction to be completed, and those issues would increase exponentially as any barrier was extended to remote and mountainous parts of the border. Large portions of the border are national parks or other protected areas. There do not seem to be significant privacy issues.

6. Is there data that can inform this decision? Are there other inputs that should have been considered?

The most relevant information would be apprehensions at the Southwest border, which have declined dramatically in recent years. Most notably, the majority of crossers are not now Mexicans, but Central Americans who are seeking humanitarian protections. Many of these crossers actually seek out Border Patrol agents to claim asylum, so they would be undeterred by a wall and would simply move to the ports of entry or find other ways to present their case to American authorities. Decisions about physical infrastructure at the border should be informed by apprehension statistics. As an example, much of the extremely remote Big Bend region does not have fencing, but it also has extremely low levels of illegal crossing. This is because it is mountainous and so remote that migrants cannot carry enough water with them to make it through the journey, and the Border Patrol is able to apprehend any border crossers as they attempt to move through the park via the few main roads. Building a wall along the border throughout the Big Bend National Park would provide very little benefit in terms of enhanced security.

7. Who will implement this, and who will oversee implementation? Does this align with the mission of the institution, or is there another entity that would be better placed to do this? What are the opportunity costs?

CBP would be responsible for building the wall, and it would be overseen by the commissioner of CBP and the secretary of DHS. There is not another entity that is better positioned to build this type of wall.

8. How will the implementation of this initiative or change be measured? What will the metrics be? Are appropriate data collections mechanisms in place to track this and determine success or failure?

These are all open questions. Apprehensions would continue to be tracked.

9. What other alternatives were considered? Are there any others that should have been considered that were not?

There are a number of alternatives that could have been considered but do not seem to have been. Most significantly, these would include expanded surveillance equipment, more sensors to detect crossings, increased flight hours for planes and drones that surveil the border and assist the Border Patrol, increased numbers of Border Patrol agents, direct assistance to Mexican authorities to help them intercept migrants at their southern border or at transit nodes near the U.S.-Mexico border, increased law enforcement operations to target the Central American gangs that are responsible for the violence that drives many Guatemalans, Hondurans, and El Salvadorans to migrate, and increased aid to those Central American countries to reduce the causes of migration.

10. Have all of the possible secondary outcomes or unintended consequences been thought through?

Clearly the answer to this is no. Spending $20 billion on a protective fence has enormous opportunity costs for other border security measures that would likely be much more effective. This would likely create a public expectation that illegal migration would be dramatically reduced or stopped, and when that does not occur there could be a great deal of public anger and backlash. To the extent that the Mexican government interprets this as a calculated insult to Mexico (which they currently do) this will do enormous harm to the U.S.-Mexico relationship and joint border security efforts. If Mexico stops detaining and removing 200,000+ Central Americans bound for the United States at their southern border every year, the flows on the U.S. Southwest border could actually end up increasing because of the wall. It is also possible that expectations of a wall could cause large amounts of potential migrants in Central America to decide that they need to get in before the wall is constructed.

11. Is there a strong political reason for this initiative?

Yes, President Trump made this a signature campaign initiative and many of his supporters feel strongly that the wall should be built at Mexico's expense. It seems unlikely that he could abandon this promise.

Travel Restrictions on Citizens of Seven Countries

1. Who are the major stakeholders in this decision, and who would stand to gain and to lose? This should include government entities, state and local communities, the private sector, and any international interests.

Citizens of the affected countries, countries whose citizens are dual nationals, airlines, American officials who are stationed in any of the affected countries, Americans who need to travel to any of the affected countries and other majority-Muslim countries more broadly.

2. Does this cost money? If so, who will pay for it? If it is going to be the federal government, will it come from appropriated funds? If so, will it come from existing appropriations or will it require new money from Congress? If it is going to be paid by a fee, who will pay the fee? Are those who will pay the fee willing to do so or will they complain?

This likely will not be expensive, as reducing the number of visas allowed and the number of travelers coming to the United States would not require new appropriated funds. If anything, this could free up funds.

3. How will Congress react? Are there any legislative changes required, both in the United States or in foreign countries, or both? Are there legislative backers for this? How long will it take for the legislation to be entered into law?

Congress seems to have split on partisan lines with a few Republican opponents. If the court challenges are sustained this may require some kind of additional legislation to be implemented, as originally contemplated.

4. How long will this last? If it is ongoing, is it self-sustaining? If it is not ongoing, is there a specific end date? If not, how will that be decided?

The order said that travel from the seven countries would be blocked for 90 days and that Syrian refugees would be blocked for 60 days, and that both would be reviewed and could be extended. The decision about whether to extend the order would be made by the president.

5. Are there any legal, privacy, or environmental issues? How will those be addressed?

There are significant legal issues and the order has currently been blocked by the Ninth Circuit Court of Appeals. There do not seem to be any major privacy or environmental issues.[6]

6. Is there data that can inform this decision? Are there other inputs that should have been considered?

This is unclear, as there are some countries that seem conspicuous in their absence from this list (such as Pakistan or Afghanistan) and in particular none of the nations that produced a 9/11 hijacker were included. In terms of specific intelligence that could have caused this to be necessary, it seems unlikely. While no one who is outside of government and does not currently hold a security clearance can know for sure that there isn't some kind of dramatic intelligence that would require this kind of suspension, we do have indications that this is not the case. A February 6, 2017 letter signed by John Kerry, the former secretary of state, Susan Rice, the former national security advisor, Avril Haines, the former deputy national security advisor, and Lisa Monaco, the former assistant to the president for counterterrorism and homeland security, stated in part: "We all agree that the United States faces real threats from terrorist networks and must take all prudent and effective steps to combat them, including the appropriate vetting of travelers to the United States. We all are nevertheless unaware of any specific threat that would justify the travel ban established by the Executive Order issued on January 27, 2017." All of them closely monitored the most sensitive intelligence produced by the Intelligence Community about these kinds of threats and left government on January 20, 2017, seven days before the executive order was issued. Therefore, if there was any dramatic new intelligence justifying this action, it would have had to have only been identified and briefed up to the president within that seven-day period.

7. Who will implement this, and who will oversee implementation? Does this align with the mission of the institution, or is there another entity that would be better placed to do this? What are the opportunity costs?

This will be implemented by DHS and the State Department, by blocking the entry of people from the identified countries and halting the issuance of new visas while revoking existing visas.

8. How will the implementation of this initiative or change be measured? What will the metrics be? Are appropriate data col-

lection mechanisms in place to track this and determine success or failure?

In the immediate term, DHS and State have systems in place that closely monitor visas and international travelers, so the implementation should be well tracked.

On a broader level, the success of any initiative like this will be related to whether there is any kind of terrorist attack that is seen to have been prevented or caused by these protections. As no traveler or national of any of these seven countries has perpetrated a terrorist attack in the United States before, it seems unlikely that one of them will do so now. This order does not appear to affect the types of attacks by ISIL-inspired terrorists that occurred in San Bernardino or Orlando, which were perpetrated by American citizens.

9. What other alternatives were considered? Are there any others that should have been considered that were not?

It appears that alternatives were not reviewed in an organized and coordinated way, and that even cabinet officials had only seen the order shortly before it was signed. Alternatives are being considered now that the executive order's implementation has been blocked in court, and it has been reported that a new draft of the order is being developed. An alternative approach would have been to actually review and improve the vetting process for individuals who are from or have traveled to these countries

10. Have all of the possible secondary outcomes or unintended consequences been thought through?

There appear to be significant secondary consequences. One of the most important is the effect on passenger targeting operations. Risk segmentation is about separating out travelers who are known to be safe so that inspection resources can be focused on people who are known to be dangerous or about whom we know too little. People holding U.S. visas have been thoroughly reviewed and are believed to be safe, which means that by making them the target of additional restrictions, we are knowingly making the pool of potentially dangerous people we are tracking less accurate. Rather than closely reviewing travel history algorithms and advance information about travelers to connect them to intelligence and law enforcement information to find unknown threats, officers will be spending their time blocking people who have already been extensively vetted and determined to not pose a threat.

There are likely to be additional consequences to U.S. relationships throughout the Muslim world, where this may be seen as implementation of the Muslim ban that was proposed during the campaign. It has been reported that this order caused celebration among jihadist groups, who view it as confirmation that the United States truly is at war with Islam.

To the extent that translators for the U.S. military have been blocked from entering the United States, this will presumably make it more difficult for the United States to find local partners for any future operations.

11. Is there a strong political reason for this initiative?

Yes, President Trump proposed a complete ban on Muslims entering the United States during the campaign and both he and congressional Republicans have repeatedly attacked the U.S. refugee program as a means for terrorists to enter the United States.

5 | Sovereignty and Twentieth-Century Border Management

It is no coincidence that the two early Trump administration policy proposals discussed in the preceding chapter focused on border management, or that they approached it from a fundamentally twentieth-century, nation-state perspective. Borders continue to be political flashpoints and border management agencies around the world are adjusting to an increasing security role. In peacetime, borders are where countries most visibly and aggressively exercise their sovereignty over national territory.

Traveler security was the area most directly implicated by 9/11, and therefore the changes to the way that passenger travel has been secured have been among the most extensive and dramatic. Rather than attempt to provide comprehensive background on all the main homeland security issues (and be much, much longer), this book will take a deep dive into border management and migration issues over the next three chapters. Showing how border management has evolved into a nation-state and now a market-state concept, and the ongoing struggles to address changing migration, will illustrate the shifts that are either underway or will need to be undertaken in other areas like cybersecurity that are not as far along in the process.

The developed world is in the midst of the second major conceptual shift in border management. The first shift was from the traditional approach to managing borders to a new paradigm in the twentieth century, and we are now moving from the twentieth-century approach to a twenty-first-century understanding of what borders mean. The next chapters will provide historical background on how border management has developed, and then discuss what twenty-first-century border management means both at and between the ports of entry, and how this new understanding of borders is profoundly affecting a number of different areas like law enforcement, industry, foreign relations, and others.

❙ The traditional approach to border management has several consistent characteristics: it focuses on customs revenue collection, pays very little attention to migration outside of significant flows that create social costs (such as a large refugee influx), lacks a consistent law enforcement presence in the border region, and relies on military force when lawlessness and things like banditry or other threats get out of hand. This is essentially the model that the United States used until the early twentieth century and is still seen in developing countries like Afghanistan, where checkpoints at transportation nodes coupled with intermittent military presence at the physical border are the main means by which flows of goods and people are controlled. This system worked reasonably well when transportation for people and goods was consolidated into a few key pathways and overall flows were small and slow, but it has been utterly overwhelmed by the explosion in travel caused first by railroads and then air travel and the proliferation of trucks and automobiles.

Historically, customs services had been better resourced and prioritized above migration agencies, for the very good reason that their duties and penalties generate a great deal of revenue for governments. The beautiful customs houses you will see at historic American port cities attest to this. Laws authorizing Alexander Hamilton's Treasury to establish the U.S. Customs Service were the fourth and fifth bills passed by the 1st Congress in 1789, but the position of commissioner of immigration wasn't created until 1891, and the position then moved among four different government departments before its responsibilities ended up in DHS.[1]

Customs also provided (and in some countries, still provides) significant opportunities for personal enrichment for unscrupulous officials. In the years leading to the American Revolution the practice of "customs racketeering" by British customs officials who would seize cargo for ostensibly legal reasons and then keep it for their own gain was widespread and a major grievance for the colonists—John Hancock, then the richest merchant in Boston, had an entire ship seized on a perjured charge in 1768, leading to riots throughout the city.[2]

The low levels of travel and the technological limitations on the threats that an individual could pose gave governments little incentive to spend large amounts of resources on enforcement at the border, and concepts of national territory were traditionally much less specifically defined than they are today. Until fairly recently travel, as distinct from migration, was almost entirely driven by trade, by the fundamental human urge to cut out the middleman and get a better deal. Travel for pleasure was an expensive and often dangerous undertaking, and was limited to the point that ancient travelers like Marco Polo or Ibn Battuta were made famous for taking journeys that would now mark them as ambitious backpackers. Many things that seem universal now, like passports and a widespread law enforcement presence at the borders, are really modern developments. Passports in modern form became widespread after the League of Nations held the Paris Conference on Passports and Customs Formalities and Through Tickets in 1920, which created standard guidelines and the booklet format we are all familiar with.[3]

Traditionally, therefore, a secure border meant that the government did a good job collecting customs fees at transit nodes and the border regions did not turn into complete badlands, although a certain level of criminality was generally expected and tacitly tolerated. If the lawlessness at the border got out of hand a government needed to be able to quickly send troops down to reassert a monopoly on force in the area.

This is how the United States used to manage the Southwest border, as exemplified by the response to Pancho Villa's attack on Columbus, New Mexico. During the Mexican Revolution, the rebel commander and criminal Pancho Villa decided to attack American interests in response to American support of Mexican president Venustiano Carranza. In 1916, Villa kidnapped and murdered 18 Americans riding on a Mexican train, and then led 1,500 guerrillas into the American border town of Columbus, New Mexico, for a raid in which 19 people were killed and the town was burnt to the ground. At this point movement across the border was an everyday occurrence with no actual enforcement at the border line, but this attack on American citizens was intolerable to the U.S. government and led President Woodrow Wilson to send General John Pershing to pursue Villa into Mexico with 10,000 troops.[4] These events show that traditional border management focused on maintaining control over the use of force within a territory and demonstrating a clear ability to respond to military or criminal threats disproportionately, rather than controlling entry or exit at the border.

Because international trade and travel were so comparatively sparse, this type of system could work pretty well. This is shown by the traditional effectiveness of the Chinese authorities at controlling the movement of goods into and out of the country by controlling the key travel nodes. Foreign traders were able to enter either overland across the Silk Road, or dock their ships at one of the very few designated trading ports near what is now Hong Kong. Contraband was smuggled in through an enormous network of bribes to key officials and an elaborate series of deceptions in which ships were docked outside of Hong Kong and everyone involved pretended the chests being brought ashore were filled with something other than opium, rather than by attempting to land illicitly up the coast at other locations to smuggle goods ashore overtly. The control exercised by the Chinese authorities was successful enough that when they eventually decided to crack down on the opium trade and prevent it from being brought ashore it led to the First Opium War, in which the British used military force to ensure that their trading ships would have access to more ports and be allowed to bring opium to the country without having to go through the complicated charade of bribery and transfers of goods. The key point is that traditional border management was fairly effective when travel and trade moved at the speed of a sailing ship or horse and were necessarily constricted to key overland roads or seaports.[5]

| That is how borders were traditionally run until things started to change in the twentieth century, when dramatic increases in the flows of goods and people, driven by technological advances and in particular the use of petroleum products as lightweight and mobile transportation fuel, overran the capacity of the old customs and migration authorities. The twentieth-century concept of border management is characterized by much more aggressive enforcement of migration, forward deployed enforcement at the jurisdictional line of the land border, visa requirements before arrival and inspection of travel documents at ports of entry, and hardened ports of entry that inspect every traveler and conveyance rather than just the movement of goods in bulk. This, again, is a relatively recent set of developments around the world and a model that is still in place in many countries.

The delineation of clearly established national borders was speeded by colonialism and competition between colonial powers that wanted to define exactly where their colonies began and those of competitors ended. Colonial officials and secret agents would spend years on travels where the main purpose was mapmaking. In one particularly dramatic example a series of British and Russian agents throughout the nineteenth century risked (and often lost) their lives on expeditions through Central Asia to demarcate the territory between Russia and India.[6] One of the results of this was a much sharper focus on exactly where national territory began and ended than had previously ever existed.

The arrival of this twentieth-century model at the land border in the United States was driven by two significant historical events. The first was in 1874 when an Illinois farmer named Joseph Glidden took out a patent for the barbed iron wire he had invented, which then first came into widespread use in Texas as a means of controlling the movement of cattle. At the very end of the nineteenth century it spread very rapidly as it allowed governments to enforce the political control of space much more quickly and cheaply than had been possible in the past.[7] Before barbed wire, blocking off hundreds of miles or more of border was an expensive and time-consuming proposition. After the invention of barbed wire, barriers could be created quickly and inexpensively to enforce the legal control of territory. This also led to a greatly increased amount of attention being paid to exactly where the physical lines of sovereign countries were located, which had in the past been much more nebulous.

The second major driver of the change in the United States was the passage of the Volstead Act in 1919, which established Prohibition. There had been small numbers of "mounted guards" who worked for the United States Immigration Service patrolling from El Paso as early as 1904, but their patrols were very limited, and with 75 total inspectors they were not able to cover much of the border. Prohibition and the accompanying explosion in bootlegging led to the formation of the Border Patrol in 1924 and the first serious investments in the ports of entry, which suddenly had a greatly increased role in inspecting for contraband. They were also charged with enforcing the limits on immigration that had recently been established by the restrictive Immigration Acts of 1921 and 1924. Once established, border control resources continued to grow.[8]

Additionally, significant changes were made in the way that international passengers were processed at sea and air ports of entry. Whereas in the past, passengers had mostly arrived by ship and could be processed in a few key locations, travelers were now spreading to different airports and moving much more quickly than had ever been possible before. Authorities responded to this by reintroducing passport requirements and establishing the necessity of visas for international travelers, who would have to visit the embassy of the country to which they intended to travel and submit to interviews and background investigations by officials of the foreign ministry before they would be given authorization to enter the country.

This could be a lengthy process, but although travel was growing faster it was generally sufficient to meet the demands from travelers.[9]

In the twentieth-century model, good border security essentially meant that authorities were forward deployed, people who attempted to cross the physical line of the border would be intercepted as they crossed, there was little or no advance information about what was coming, international travelers went through visa interviews conducted by foreign ministry officials, and there was often very little communication between authorities on either side of the border. The really iconic and most extreme twentieth-century image of this kind of border control was the Berlin Wall, where it was incredibly dangerous to cross illegally and all controlled crossings were through military checkpoints. The authorities on either side had essentially no communication or cooperation and there was no warning of when someone might attempt to cross illicitly between the ports of entry. If security is measured by assets at the physical line of the border, then border security tends to be measured by the level of visible enforcement resources. Security then means more stuff between the ports and slower processing at the ports, so that security and facilitation are in direct competition, or in the language that officials used to use, are "balanced." This implied that the more officers physically standing on the line, the more onerous the physical inspections at the ports of entry, and the greater the transaction costs to move across the line, the more secure the border was. Basically, a country would decide how much disruption of trade and travel and enforcement presence it was politically willing to handle, and received a corresponding level of security.

The increased enforcement presences at borders and the disconnect between authorities on opposing sides also led to the function of borders as political flashpoints, where larger disagreements and conflicts between neighboring countries were sparked due to the constant interaction between populations and authorities. This meant that security incidents generally result in closed or dramatically restricted borders. This occurred after 9/11, as international flights were grounded and inspections at the U.S. land borders were made strenuous enough to effectively shut down the regular flows of people and goods. In another example that more pointedly shows the political tension around the border, in 1985 the former commissioner of customs, William Van Raab, shut the Southwest border for four days after the torture and murder of DEA agent Enrique "Kiki" Camarena, in which some Mexican authorities were complicit.

These kinds of responses exact enormous economic costs on both countries, quickly run up against the requirements of travel and commerce, and cannot be sustained.

The specific location of the international boundary became much more important than it had been under the traditional model of border management, because in order to be forward deployed on the border authorities have to know exactly where their territory begins and ends. Much of the border between the United States and Mexico is based on a river that has shifted repeatedly in the past and moved tracts of land from the bank on one country's side to the other. As settlements would be established along the rivers, the question of whether sovereignty shifted as a river moved gained increased importance. To resolve these issues, in 1889 the United States and Mexico created the International Boundary and Water Commission, which works bilaterally to determine the exact location of the international boundary and to manage the flows and use of waterways that touch both countries. This commission has become a model for how two countries can address potentially contentious issues about the border and especially rights to different flows of water in the dry Southwest region through bilateral coordination and without conflict.

Because security and facilitation are in conflict in this model, there is always an extreme amount of pressure on officers to reduce the security of their inspections in order to speed the overall throughput. This was seen in the United States when the Visa Waiver Program was implemented without a system put into place to provide any sort of check that would be commensurate with the information compiled on a visa application. This made international travel from countries in the program much faster and easier, but at the cost of a specific reduction in the security screening of travelers bound for the United States.

In the twentieth-century model of border management, the work done at the border is also largely separated from efforts to combat organized crime or terrorism. Efforts to interdict contraband at the border were independent of the long-term investigations done by law enforcement officials, whose ultimate goal was always arrest and prosecution. Investigators often prevented border agents from stopping known criminals or contraband, preferring to let them enter the country so that they would not be aware that they were under suspicion and could then be followed by investigators while a criminal case was built.

The twentieth-century model of border management leaves authorities one chance to stop a threatening person—when they physically cross the border and are inspected. This means that officers processing large quantities of traffic often have no more than a minute to rely on their instincts and training to make a decision about admissibility. In the minute that a border officer interacts with a crosser, absent a very compelling reason to order further inspection, there is no way for an officer to act on every possible concern without dramatically slowing throughput. The result of this was that generally stopping threats relied on either extremely unusual behavior from crossers or extraordinary perceptiveness from officers.

Two of the most significant examples of successes in stopping terrorists at the border before 9/11 actually demonstrate this phenomenon clearly. The first is Ahmed Ressam, better known as the attempted Millennium Bomber, who planned to detonate a fertilizer bomb at Los Angeles International Airport. Ressam crossed into the United States from Canada by ferry at Port Angeles, Washington, with the bomb in the wheel well of his vehicle. Ressam was visibly sick and was uncooperative with officers, which caused Customs Inspector Diana Dean to order a second inspection of his car because he was acting "hinky." Officers then found the explosive material, which they initially thought to be drugs, concealed in the wheel well. His arrest was largely due to the alertness and intuition of his inspecting officer. Additionally, he was the last car to come off the ferry, which meant that the officers were under no pressure because there was no line behind him to hurry his processing.[10]

The second example is Mohamed al Khatani, a highly trained al Qaeda operative who intended to participate in the September 11 attacks and was detained at the Orlando airport in August 2001 after arriving on a flight from London. While Mohammed Atta, the leader of the hijackers, waited upstairs in the airport, al Khatani was sent to secondary inspection because of his refusal to speak any English at the primary inspection booth. There, the inspector conducting his interview, Jose Melendez-Perez, was so concerned by his inconsistent answers to basic questions and aggressive demeanor that he recommended to his supervisor that entry be refused. Because relations with Saudi Arabia were seen as extremely sensitive and Saudi travelers were rarely denied, the decision had to go to the assistant port director for approval. Eventually, al Khatani was denied entry and returned to London, with the result that there were four hijackers on Flight 93, where passengers were able to overcome the hijackers and crash the plane into a field in Pennsylvania rather than its intended target (likely the Capitol or the White House), instead of the five hijackers that were on each of the other three flights.[11]

In both of these examples the professionalism and skill of the customs officers prevented or impeded terrorist attacks. This, however, shows the inadequacy of the twentieth-century approach against groups like al Qaeda—a country cannot rely on heroic efforts from border officers to stop threats. They should be the last line of defense against terrorist travel rather than the first and only line. For the one 9/11 hijacker who was stopped because of his extremely unusual behavior, 19 were able to enter the United States legally, and had the Millennium Bomber not been sick, uncooperative, or the last person to leave the ferry, he may well have succeeded in his planned attack on Los Angeles International Airport.

The twentieth-century approach to border management also resulted in huge disincentives to information sharing between intelligence and law enforcement. Prosecutions require evidence that can be presented and challenged in court, while intelligence agencies require that their information and its sources remain protected. The result was that sharing information outside of the rigid existing channels could jeopardize major cases. This is shown clearly in the prosecution of the al Qaeda embassy bombings in east Kenya and Tanzania, where contact between the FBI's intelligence and criminal investigation teams endangered the admissibility of evidence and required the attorney general to personally intervene to save the case.[12] Making a cabinet official deal with your mistake is one of the great disasters that can befall a Washington bureaucrat. Sharing information outside of regulations could be devastating for an official's career and even result in possible criminal liability if it wasn't disclosed, as making false statements to the FISA courts risked felony prosecution.[13] The result of this was shown dramatically when the FBI actually possessed and shared intelligence with other criminal investigators about a 9/11 participant before the attacks but then had to pull the information back and say that it shouldn't have been shared.[14]

Many of these laws and processes were implemented after the intelligence scandals of the 1970s, and were thoughtful and appropriate responses to the strategic context of the time. They were horribly matched, however, to respond to the threat presented by the market-state terrorist group al Qaeda.

6 | Risk Management and Twenty-First-Century Borders

Border management has now evolved into a third distinct phase. The twenty-first-century model of border management that began after 9/11 sees borders as more than mere lines separating countries where all enforcement efforts should be focused, but instead as international flows of people and goods. American authorities have had to adapt their efforts to match this reality—focusing exclusively on the border itself would be a wholly inadequate method of addressing threats and protecting the country.

Several recent events have further demonstrated the inadequacy of the twentieth-century approach to border management to address modern terrorist threats. These attack attempts demonstrate how quickly terrorist threats are evolving and attempting to exploit weaknesses within the screening system. This has been proven by incidents like the Christmas Day bomber, who had been identified as a target for secondary inspection but, had he succeeded, would have downed a U.S.-bound airliner before he arrived. This was further shown by the Yemen cargo plot, where explosives disguised as printer cartridges destined for the United States were intercepted in the United Kingdom, but not before they had been carried on passenger airlines. We now understand that operations at and between the ports of entry need to be driven by assessments of risk and closely connected to international and domestic intelligence and law enforcement. These are briefly described below, as understanding how they were conducted and the vulnerabilities that they demonstrated is helpful to understand why our current regime looks the way it does. These are the particular terrorist attempts and attacks:

- 2001—Richard Reid, the shoe bomber who used a match to attempt to ignite a bomb concealed in the sole of his shoe on a flight from Paris to the United States. He was only stopped by other passengers who physically restrained him, and investigations after the incident showed that the bomb in his shoe would have been sufficient to down the plane. Significantly, he was a Caucasian convert to Islam who used his status as a citizen of a Visa Waiver Program country to evade further scrutiny. This both demonstrates the inadequacy of ethnic profiling to identify terrorist operatives and showed the need for better advance information about individuals from visa waiver countries, which led to the Electronic System for Travel Authorization (known as ESTA, which will be further described later in this chapter).[1]

- 2006—A terrorist cell based in the United Kingdom attempted to use liquid explosives concealed in sports drink bottles to blow up aircraft bound for the United States and Canada in flight, which was discovered by British police after an extensive surveillance operation of the terrorist network led to the arrests of 24 suspects.[2]

- 2009—Umar Farouk Abdulmutallab, known as the underwear or Christmas Day bomber, who flew from Nigeria to Amsterdam and then to Detroit, where he attempted to ignite a bomb concealed in his underwear on the plane. He was only stopped by the vigilance of other passengers who saw him attempting to ignite the explosive and intervened. Abdulmutallab had been flagged on the CBP systems for secondary screening when he arrived in Detroit. This, obviously, was too late to prevent him from attempting to blow up the airliner, and showed the need for better systems to prevent watch-listed individuals from boarding planes bound for the United States in the first place.[3]

- 2010—Faisal Shazad, the Times Square bomber, who attempted to detonate a car filled with explosives in New York and then flee the country by flying to Dubai. He was identified by CBP by connecting a cell phone number to the advance passenger information that airlines submitted when he attempted to board a plane.[4]

- 2011—The Yemen cargo plot, in which al Qaeda on the Arabian Peninsula operatives concealed bombs in printer cartridges that they planned to detonate in cargo planes over Chicago. This demonstrated the inadequate analysis of information about air cargo before it was boarded on U.S.-bound planes, and led to the development of the Air Cargo Advance Screening program, which is discussed below.[5]

The key to addressing these threats is through risk segmentation and intelligence-based law enforcement. In order to segment things and people by risk levels, you have to be able to separate them out before they arrive at the port, which means know who or what they are before they get to the border. The new approach means that risk segmentation actually processes legitimate goods and travel more quickly while providing better security.

Balanced solutions to twenty-first-century threats are possible but are difficult to find. With traveler security, authorities have now moved beyond the idea of an inverse relationship between security and trade facilitation, and instead now understand that they are directly correlated. Better security means faster processing and fewer inspections. Security does not mean getting one chance to intercept a dangerous person or contraband when they physically cross the border, but now means focusing on entire supply chains and travel flows to intercept threats before they arrive at our ports of entry. Advance information through trusted traveler and shipper programs is an essential element in this. The more information that officers are able to review ahead of time, the better they are able to separate out traffic based on the amount of attention it requires from inspectors. CBP is able to process a member of Global Entry traveling to the United States by plane in most cases in under two minutes total, faster than the "Diplomats" line.

This shift has significant implications that will continue to manifest themselves around the world. Immediately after 9/11, the U.S. government emphasized "pushing the border out," so that inspections were conducted at foreign points of departure and threats could be stopped before they leave for the United States. The twenty-first-century concept of border management takes this one step further, so that threats are not just identified by U.S. officials before their last point of departure toward America, but can be identified using advance information and partnership with industry at key points throughout the supply chain and travel paths, at which point they can be acted upon and stopped by whichever law enforcement authority has jurisdiction. This means that DHS is not just looking to get an additional chance at inspection before someone or something arrives at the physical border, but is instead making it harder for any dangerous person or item to exploit legal flows of trade and travel around the world.

In addition to being inadequate to address the threat posed by international terrorist travel, twentieth-century border management is even more unequal to threats such as transnational organized crime, human trafficking, and narcotics smuggling. By using advance information and applying targeting and algorithms to identify high-risk individuals, officers at the ports of entry can be much more effective than they were able to be in the past. As an example, a human trafficker who arrives at a port of entry with a young child he claims is his niece may not necessarily provoke a great deal of scrutiny if an officer only encounters him once and can't immediately see his travel history, but if the officer at migration control is able to see that he has entered the country with two other young girls he also claimed were his nieces on previous occasions and that his travel history involves countries designated as high risk for human trafficking by the State Department, the officer is much more likely to stop the criminal. Relatedly, while an officer at the land border might not identify an individual as a likely narcotics smuggler based on normal indicators, if she is able to see that the individual previously crossed three times in the same vehicle as a member of the Barrio Azteca gang, she can ensure that the crosser receives a secondary inspection. Under the twentieth-century model, there would have been little chance of intercepting these threats at the border.

| In order to effectively separate travelers by the level of risk that they may pose, information must be collected in advance, reviewed, and used in a risk determination, and then matched to an individual traveler who is processed appropriately before departure and on arrival. The United States has now put the key elements in place for this system and is working to extend them to partner countries around the world.

The elements that were put together in response to these threats and which are essential to twenty-first-century border management are as follows:

- Advance information about travelers bound for the United States before they depart, so that dangerous people can be identified before they board planes and either be put through additional screening or be kept from boarding.
- A consolidated database of potentially dangerous individuals that generates watch lists that are used for anyone attempting to enter the country, whether through air, land, or sea ports of entry.

- Capability to quickly run information about travelers against the databases and watch lists and to use algorithms to identify anomalous and potentially concerning patterns, what law enforcement refers to as "targeting."
- Biometric identification about travelers—which includes capturing biometrics when they enter a country, comparing these biometrics to existing databases, and securely storing this information on passports or other travel documents so that imposters can be immediately identified.
- "Smart" travel documents that are difficult to counterfeit and can carry electronic information about travelers, as well as a consolidated international database of lost and stolen documents—which is currently maintained by Interpol.
- A trusted traveler regime that allows frequent, safe travelers to be separated out of the flow of traffic for expedited processing.
- Applying the lessons of counterterrorism efforts to work against transnational criminal organizations, in particular through a modernized program of information sharing and coordinated efforts across agencies to deny criminal infrastructure to illicit organizations.

Combined, these allow law enforcement to identify and stop threats. All of these elements, their importance, and their implementation are discussed in more detail in the sections below.

❙ Any risk segmentation regime begins with collecting information about travelers before they arrive at the border. The actual inspection by an officer upon arrival should be a backstop for vetting done before arrival, rather than the primary security screening of a traveler. In this model, security and facilitation are not in competition but are two outcomes of the same set of circumstances, since security doesn't just mean spending more time on an inspection. Advance information allows CBP to speed passenger processing while being much more effective at identifying threats. One of the key outcomes of this approach is that security does not need to be just an unwanted economic burden for industry, but can actually have direct economic benefits as well. Central to this has been the expanded collection of advance information about goods and people bound for the United States. By using targeting rules against this information earlier in the process, DHS is able to stop threats at foreign departure points before they get on conveyances. Advance information is also used to prevent dangerous people from boarding domestic flights. Some of the most important programs to collect advance information and background about how they were established and their effects are discussed below.

The Electronic System for Traveler Authorization (ESTA) was established in 2007 to address a gap in information about travelers from Visa Waiver countries, and was based on a program developed by the government of Australia. While the Visa Waiver Program has obvious facilitation benefits and increases travel flows, eliminating visas removed the most significant opportunity for the U.S. government to vet travelers to the United States and identify concerns. This also was based on the assumption that citizens or residents of countries like France or Germany were less likely to be terrorists than other travelers, which has been repeatedly dramatically disproved by the 9/11 attacks, the Charlie Hedbo, Nice, Bataclan, and Berlin attacks, and the large numbers of foreign fighters who have traveled to Syria from Western Europe and in many cases returned without the knowledge of authorities. Once the program had been created, dangerous travelers from Visa Waiver countries could only be identified after they arrived for primary processing at the airports. After 9/11, it was clear that U.S. agencies needed more time to identify potential threats and to connect the dots on individuals who may have intended harm. ESTA requires any U.S.-bound travelers to submit an online authorization request three days before their travel to the United States. This program has now been seen to be a clear success and is being replicated in other places around the world. Canada implemented their equivalent, which is called eTA, in 2015.

Passenger Name Record data is the information collected by airlines when a reservation is made, and Advance Passenger Information is the information gathered when individuals check in for flights. Airlines collect this information about passengers but they did not previously share this information with federal officials. Key elements of this information are submitted to DHS before the flight. This information is also used to track when people exit the United States as well.

Trucks are required to submit their manifests an hour before arrival at the land border, which provides CBP with some time to target and assess the risk of the shipment. Members of CBP's trusted shipper program are able to submit their manifests a half hour in advance of crossing, which is one of the benefits provided to participants. Notably, there is no advance information required for people crossing the land border, either as pedestrians or in passenger vehicles. This limits the effectiveness of CBP's targeting efforts on these individuals, and at some point in the future a requirement to submit information electronically in advance of crossing will likely need to be established. It would be possible to structure this in the form of an appointment system, where people who had submitted their information in advance are allowed to cross quickly while passengers showing up without providing prior information go through more involved screening.

The Air Cargo Advanced Screening program, or ACAS, which was established jointly by CBP and TSA in the wake of the Yemen printer cartridge bomb plot, is probably the most important example of how government and industry can work jointly to secure supply chains, and it provides a model for future programs. The Yemen cargo plot made it clear that the amount of advance information about air cargo that DHS was receiving and analyzing, which focused on identifying concerning cargo so that it could be inspected after it arrived in the United States, was inadequate to prevent dangerous situations. Traditionally, the response would have been for the department to meet internally, decide what information would be most useful to detect these kinds of plots, and then create a requirement for industry with penalties for noncompliance.

That was not the approach that CBP and TSA used in this case. Instead, they approached industry from the outset and asked the cargo carriers to look at the information that was already being collected for logistical purposes and to identify elements that could be provided to CBP and TSA before packages were shipped to the United States. They then jointly developed a pilot program, which has since been made permanent, that allows CBP and TSA to review information about packages before they are put on planes. This allows them to identify threats and keep them from being loaded, and to do all of this with information that the carriers were already collecting for the sake of efficiency. Notably, this also allows CBP to speed the processing of safe cargo after it has arrived, resulting in a benefit both to government and the companies involved. The interests of security and expediting trade were demonstrated to be two sides of the same process rather than in conflict.

| One of the key recommendations of the 9/11 Commission was to break down the barriers to information sharing between different security agen-

cies so information that could prevent an attack would not be hoarded by different officials. The institutional incentives for law enforcement, especially investigative agencies, are against sharing information, since any information passed to another agency could cause another agency to take action that might negatively affect (or steal) your case, or could result in administrative or even criminal penalties.

The 9/11 attacks made it clear that this approach was inadequate to meet twenty-first-century threats, and the incentives have now been changed so that anyone who has information about a possible terrorist attack now fears that their career could be ended if they do *not* share it, rather than the opposite situation that existed before.

The new watch-listing regime established after 9/11 ensures that information on any known and suspected terrorists is collected in a central location and put onto a common list that allows information to flow between law enforcement and intelligence agencies (with appropriate safeguards).[6] Terrorist identities are collected in what is called the Terrorist Identities Datamart Environment, or TIDE, which was designated as the "central and shared knowledge bank on known and suspected terrorists and international terror groups" by the Intelligence Reform and Terrorism Prevention Act of 2004. Information from TIDE is then nominated to be included on the consolidated watch list, the Terrorist Screening Database (TSDB), which is maintained by the FBI's Terrorist Screening Center.

At the border, CBP uses an information sharing platform called TECS,[7] which used to stand for the Treasury Enforcement Communications System but stopped being an acronym when Customs was moved into CBP as part of DHS. TECS allows officers to quickly check individuals against a central terrorism watch list as well as criminal databases, previous travel history, and law enforcement lookouts.

The centralized identities in TIDE and the TSDB have been incredibly important in ensuring that dangerous people are stopped at the border or prevented from ever boarding flights bound for the United States, which is done by telling the airline to deny boarding. While it was difficult to work through the legal and policy issues to allow this information to be collected in a single place, and some agencies were forced to share information that they might rather have kept to themselves to build cases, these costs are vastly overshadowed by the benefits of ensuring that possible terrorist travel is quickly and accurately identified and stopped. Significantly, the U.S. government does not have a comparable central database of criminal information, meaning that information on cartel members and other extremely dangerous people may be located in investigative case files that are not shared with officers at the border. This situation and the possible application of lessons learned from the counterterrorism mission successes to organized crime are discussed further below.

❚ Biometric identification is an essential component of twenty-first-century border management, to prevent document fraud and verify travelers' identities. Biometrics allow an officer at the border to be sure that she is interacting with the person who was run through databases and watch lists based on their advance information, and therefore both speeds processing and enhances security. After 9/11, CBP began collecting two and then 10 fingerprints from travelers.

The U.S. government maintains three primary groups of biometric identities:

- Travelers biometrics collected by CBP during processing at the ports of entry. This database is maintained by DHS's Office of Biometric Identity Management, and tracks all of the different encounters that DHS has with travelers. This allows DHS to determine if someone is using an alias or fraudulent identification.[8]
- Biometrics collected by federal, state, or local law enforcement databases, and consolidated by the FBI into the Integrated Automated Fingerprint Identification System (referred to as IAFIS, pronounced eye-aye-fis).
- Information collected by Defense internationally, which would include things like fingerprints done of captured enemy combatants or found during investigation of a roadside bomb.

By running travelers quickly against these three datasets, CBP is much more quickly and effectively able to identify potential threats at the border than they had been previously.

CBP is testing new technology using iris scans and facial recognition that could dramatically reduce the processing time at ports of entry by allowing travelers to be identified and reviewed as they walk through airports, although there are significant questions about how this would be linked to current requirements and the privacy impact of this kind of technology that are unresolved. In order to implement this kind of system the government would necessarily have to collect and store extremely sensitive information and resolve questions about the scope of how it would be used and shared with other agencies.

Importantly, the United States does not have the ability to collect complete information about who is exiting the country, and almost no ability to verify the biometrics of people leaving. As a result, it is very difficult to identify people who overstay their visas. This has been identified repeatedly as a security gap that needs to be addressed—including by means of legislation with requirements to develop a comprehensive exit verification system—but the logistical barriers to this point have been insurmountable. DHS officials refer to this problem as "Entry/Exit," although it is really exit screening that is the major issue.

Currently the United States verifies exits by using airline reservation data, which provides basic information about everyone booked on a flight out. There is no mechanism to verify that every person who makes a reservation actually leaves, or to have an official verify the identification of a person getting on a flight. As a result, DHS has exit information that it is fairly confident in but not certain of for about 90 percent of the individuals exiting the United States. Some countries, like the Netherlands, do verify everyone who leaves and has them pass through a customs/migration check, but their airports are configured to make this a straightforward process. American airports were not designed to do this, so moving the vast numbers of passengers leaving the country back through CBP processing or through new processing centers would require a large-scale redesign of all of the major American airports. The alternative, of having CBP officers at every gate with international flights checking the identities of outbound passengers, would require an enormous increase in CBP staffing and deployment of mobile biometric technology and make boarding a much slower and more onerous process than it currently is. Any passengers whose review raises issues that need to be resolved would either have to miss their flight or delay takeoff, even if it is a matter of resolving a name match with some kind of criminal suspect. This would also result in a larger number of people who are not terrorists but who have some kind of other flag, such as an outstanding warrant, being identified and pulled off of planes. From a law enforcement perspective this is a good thing, although for the airlines and other passengers it could cause major delays. In the end, though, some kind of system is going to have to be established at airports, and the hope of officials is that advances in biometric technology can make this as streamlined as possible. The privacy implications of this, whether through facial recognition or iris scanning or some other biometric capture method, will be extremely difficult to balance.

The logistics are even more daunting at the land borders, where almost no exit information is captured and where there is little infrastructure in place to do outbound inspections. The outbound inspections that are done now are mostly focused on illicit flows of firearms and bulk cash across the Southwest border, rather than verifying that, say, a student visa holder has left within the allotted time of their visa. In order to establish a comprehensive outbound inspection system at the land border, enormous new investments would need to be made in inspection infrastructure, essentially doubling the footprint of existing ports of entry. Because ports of entry were designed to inspect only entries and many of them are located in urban areas, this expansion would likely cost tens of billions of dollars and run into significant eminent domain and environmental issues, and be violently opposed by border communities and industry.

The long-term solution to this vulnerability at the land border clearly lies in establishing bilateral entry/exit systems, where a person leaving the United States is inspected by Canada or Mexico and their information is then simultaneously transmitted to American officials. This would be much less onerous than trying to duplicate the inbound inspection infrastructure, and takes advantage of the fact that Canadian and Mexican officials already have the capability to conduct inspections of every person leaving the United States at a land border. By transmitting information that American officials already have the authority to collect, this kind of program would avoid unnecessary and time-consuming duplication. Pilot programs to establish this system with both Canada and Mexico have begun and will hopefully lead to permanent programs.

| A twenty-first-century border management regime requires secure travel documents that are extremely hard to counterfeit. DHS has increased the security standards for American passports and for those of travelers to the United States, with the result that passengers can be processed more quickly and securely at the ports of entry.

In 2006, DHS launched the Western Hemisphere Travel Initiative, which has demonstrated how security and facilitation are two parts of the same processes. Security features were strengthened on driver's licenses and other approved smart travel documents, and these then allowed faster crossing at the land borders. Securely storing information about travelers on these documents and transmitting them sooner in the crossing process gives officers more time to make an accurate risk determination, which in turn means that safe travelers can be processed more quickly.

❙ Targeting has become the central feature of twenty-first-century border management, and has become the means by which risk management principles are applied practically at the border. After 9/11, new requirements for advance information from industry and travelers created a significant data management problem for the newly merged CBP. To address this and better identify threats, the agency established the National Targeting Center, which was later split into cargo and passenger functions. These centers take the enormous amount of advance data and use rule searches, algorithms, comprehensive reviews against intelligence and law enforcement databases, and an ongoing process of forensic analysis to continually improve their ability to identify threats within the streams of legitimate trade and travel. Watch officers are responding to potential matches of advance passenger information against terrorist and criminal watch lists and reviewing travel and cargo movements for suspicious patterns.

This means that for cargo and passengers, CBP is able to identify many threats long before they actually arrive at American ports. This both allows CBP to stop dangerous people and things before they depart and to more effectively target inspection resources after arrival. The benefits in this approach for security and for customs revenue collection are pretty obvious and other countries have begun establishing their own targeting enterprises. Mexico in particular has made impressive progress with their cargo targeting center in Queretaro. Mexico Customs has now gone from having 90 percent of their inspections done randomly a few years ago to now having 90 percent done based on analysis of advance information.

The trend of increasing automation is making risk segmentation more efficient in a number of different areas. There's a term you hear a lot in law enforcement when you talk about data management, which is to "fat finger" something. Fat fingering is basically any laborious process where information has to be entered or processed, and it evokes an image of a burly law enforcement officer glumly pecking away at a keyboard. Generally, you want law enforcement officers to do as little fat fingering as is possible, because their time is valuable (they're more expensive than other federal employees) and they don't like and aren't particularly good at data entry. There are lots of different tasks at the border that have had to be done by the equivalent of fat fingering, and as DHS is able to increasingly automate these, officers are being freed up to spend more time on the kind of analysis and investigations that provide the greatest benefit for their time.

One of the important ways automation is changing operations is through the use of automated kiosks at primary processing, which can now be seen at airports around the country. Rather than spending their time physically scanning passports and reviewing the information, officers are able to spend more time conducting interviews and secondary inspections of people who pose a known risk or about whom they know less. This also has the benefit of making overall processing faster.

There are a number of areas like this where automation will continue to multiply law enforcement effectiveness. There are situations like when hits on targeting rules have to be adjudicated individually by officers to make sure names really match, or when images from nonintrusive inspection equipment have to be reviewed individually by officers, which are likely places where increased automation will allow officers to spend their time much more effectively. Doing criminal link analysis, reviewing X-rays, and scanning passports at primary screening are all areas where automation will likely fundamentally change the existing staffing-intensive processes.

| One of the most important advances in risk segmentation has been the development of what are called trusted traveler and trusted shipper programs. To use an analogy from former assistant secretary Alan Bersin, if the problem for border authorities is to identify the dangerous needle within the haystack of legal trade and travel, trusted traveler and shipper programs reduce the size of the haystack that must be searched by separating out people and goods that are known to require less scrutiny. As a result of this, a CBP officer at the Southwest border is able to quickly process daily shipments of auto parts from a major car company that submits to voluntary security inspections of their factory facilities and spend more time on a truck full of produce from Sinaloa operated by an independent and unknown company. Officers have always had to prioritize their inspection efforts, but these programs allow them to do it much more sys-

tematically and with greater confidence that they are focusing their efforts on the right targets. Of course, in order for these programs to truly be secure, their members must be continuously vetted against law enforcement databases and be subject to less frequent random inspections to ensure that they stay honest.

These programs both speed the movement of lawful trade and travel and enhance security at the same time, because these are complementary aims. Officers who do not have to waste time on routine processing of safe travel are able to spend more time on potentially dangerous crossings, which makes their efforts more effective and helps better secure the flows of goods and people across the border. Because of this, DHS leadership has identified increasing membership in these programs as a homeland security imperative, and there are now millions of members of the various programs.

There are several different trusted traveler and trader programs operated by DHS for different types of crossers. Global Entry, which is CBP's trusted traveler program for international air passengers, is now in operation at all major U.S. airports and has over five million members. It allows participants to use electronic kiosks and complete their customs and migration processing in as little as a few minutes. Membership has been extended to citizens of partner countries with reciprocal programs. Global Entry members are actually generally processed faster than any other travelers, including the V.I.P. and Diplomats lines at certain airports. This program is probably the single most popular thing about DHS.

At the land border with Mexico there is the Secure Electronic Network for Travelers Rapid Inspection (SENTRI), which U.S. and Mexican citizens can join and which has dedicated lanes at many of the major ports of entry, so that members are separated out from the regular traffic to cross more quickly. The program also uses radio frequency identification technology (RFID) within the documents to transmit traveler information to CBP officers before they arrive at the inspection booths. Certain locations even have SENTRI only bridges, which make crossing even faster. The U.S.–Canadian trusted traveler program is called NEXUS, which doesn't actually stand for anything and operates both at airports and land ports of entry. NEXUS also uses RFID technology at the land border. CBP also has dedicated lanes at the land border that are only for travelers with RFID technology, which are called READY lanes, and which move more quickly than the overall traffic.

TSA's Precheck program extended the trusted traveler concept to passengers boarding flights in the United States, including for purely domestic travel, and has become extremely popular since its introduction. Members have shorter lines, faster processing, and do not have to do things like remove their shoes or take laptops out of bags. Global Entry members are automatically granted Precheck membership. Incidentally, given that Global Entry costs $100 and Precheck alone costs $85, it's a better deal to join Global Entry and just get both programs, unless you are absolutely positive that you will not be traveling internationally for the next five years.

In early 2018, CBP had agreements with the Netherlands, South Korea, Australia, and the United Kingdom to allow reciprocal access to their trusted traveler programs. This is sure to continue expanding, as more countries are recognizing the obvious benefits of these programs and are working to establish them based on the U.S. model.

CBP's flagship trusted shipper program is the awkwardly named Customs–Trade Partnership Against Terrorism, or C-TPAT. Participants provide significant amounts of security information about their business processes and agree to have their facilities around the world inspected periodically by U.S. officials. In exchange, they receive fewer inspections and are provided other facilitation benefits when their goods are processed by CBP. There are three tiers within the program to recognize different levels of security, and nearly all of the large companies involved in cross-border commerce have become members. This program has been effective because it aligns the priorities of industry and government. Companies have strong interests in keeping their supply chains secure for purely economic reasons, so when government is able to verify the steps that companies have taken and to use this knowledge to process their goods more quickly at the border, both sides benefit.

CBP has an additional program for truck drivers called Free and Secure Trade, or FAST. Just like with trusted traveler programs, FAST trucks are processed more quickly and receive fewer inspections. The ports of entry with the largest cargo volume all have dedicated lanes for FAST drivers, and the extent to which the lanes are separated out from the rest of the traffic has a strong effect on overall throughput. The World Trade Bridge in Laredo, for example, has a dedicated FAST lane that extends entirely across the bridge over the Rio Grande and allows trusted traffic to cross more quickly without joining the general truck line, which is a significant part of the appeal of the crossing to industry.

The effectiveness of these programs has been recognized around the world, and the World Customs Organization is strongly encouraging their development and expansion (they refer to the programs as Authorized Economic Operator programs, rather than trusted trader or shipper). Canada and Mexico have trusted trader programs that now offer reciprocal membership with their U.S. equivalents for companies that agree to have their information shared with the other governments.

| The interaction between government and industry at the border is one of the areas that is changing the fastest. For industry, twenty-first-century border management means that they have a much bigger responsibility for ensuring security and compliance. As a government, it generally means that agencies are moving to an account-based, rather than transaction-based, regime, which has important benefits for industry. CBP's Centers of Excellence and Expertise, which have been established in 10 locations around the country (e.g., centers on petroleum in Houston, textiles in San Francisco, automotive in Detroit), provide a centralized group of experts and a point of contact for companies for all of their interactions with the agency. This means that companies do not have to depend on the Port of Eagle Pass having an expert in processing say, pharmaceuticals, and can instead interact directly with the same experts for all of their transactions.

This is an important example of moving beyond the traditional regulator/industry dynamic, where government would impose requirements and companies would either spend the money to meet them or be penalized. Companies in many cases collect much more detailed information for logistical reasons than security agencies would traditionally request. The government will move increasingly to partnering with companies to provide security standards and provide assistance in reaching them, and at the same time ensuring compliance through random inspections throughout the supply chain.

The long-awaited establishment of what is called a single window (where information about imported goods can be entered electronically for all relevant government agencies) and the reduction in transaction costs that will accompany it is enormously important. CBP acts as the executive agent for 47 different agencies at the border, all of which want some kind of information from traders, and most of which have different forms they require the information on. The single window will provide a central electronic portal to enter this information. This is something that has been in development for a long time, and by a long time I mean that it was announced in 1995 in a memorandum by Vice President Al Gore, but it has been moving much more rapidly in the last years because in February 2014 President Obama issued an executive order requiring all agencies to be on the system by December 2016, which they largely managed to do. This is a technical area that doesn't get the attention it probably deserves, but the benefits this would bring to industry are comparable to what will come from a major trade agreement. The longer term next step once this is implemented will be to harmonize our single window with Mexico's and Canada's.

The physical infrastructure at North American land borders is the least modern part of the border management enterprise, and the difficulty and time involved in updating it have blocked innovations in processing cross-border traffic. America's border crossings, which are several decades old on average and designed well before post-9/11 security requirements, were not planned for the volumes of trade and travel that they currently process. This is not just an issue that affects the border region; these crossings are national economic assets and are a major gateway for American exports, as Canada and Mexico are America's largest export partners. Border-crossing traffic tends to be funneled to a small number of very large crossings, and at peak times cars and trucks can wait for hours to cross.

A great deal of additional work will need to be done to address the full deficit of investment. All efforts should be made to improve throughput using existing infrastructure and to modernize border processing, but even if those efforts were to result in a 50 percent improvement in wait times across both land borders, the infrastructure would still be in dire need of updating. CBP has identified a $5 billion deficit in improvements to existing infrastructure alone, and when combined with the high priority new projects that have been identified through the Department of Transportation's regional master planning process, relying on the traditional appropriated funds clearly will be inadequate.

There are three essential steps that must be taken to fix America's border infrastructure. First, the planning processes with Mexico and Canada must be made fully binational. Second, greater financial resources are going to have to be found for these projects, whether through direct investment or through regulatory changes that make it possible to attract more private funding. Third, better use must be made of existing infrastructure by moving processes that are not essential for security out of the ports of entry and away from the border.*

Container Security

Cargo container security is still an enormous challenge and the steps that have been taken since 9/11 have been much less comprehensive than the improvements in passenger screening. I have personal interests in this topic: when I left government I cofounded a company to develop autonomous systems such as aerial drones for container inspections. The scale of seaborne shipping is staggering: a single cargo container has the approximate size and internal complexity of a moving truck for a single family home, and it can take five officers three hours to thoroughly inspect one.[9] Approximately 12 million unique containers enter the United States each year, mostly through seaports, some multiple times.[10] The main ports of entry for sea cargo are located in some of the country's most populated urban areas (e.g., Los Angeles, Seattle, Newark, Miami, and New Orleans). Most containers receive no inspection at all after they pass briefly through radiation portal monitors. CBP identifies around 5 percent as high-risk and uses X-ray-type devices to image them, and then conducts physical searches if anything suspicious is identified from the images.[11]

The systems that move goods around the world are remarkably stateless and unregulated. The English author Rose George, after researching a book about shipping and riding as a passenger on a cargo ship, concluded that "in practice the ocean is the world's wildest place."[12] Ship ownership is largely hidden. When the tanker *Erika*, which was carrying oil for the French company Total, crashed in 1999, authorities had to work through 12 layers of shell companies to find the beneficial owner.[13] The ships themselves have "flags of convenience," and are, on paper, based in countries like Liberia, Panama, and Sierra Leone.[14] This avoids regulation and means they are not subject to the developed world's labor laws, and the ships are

---

* I have written extensively about this elsewhere. Those interested can see Ben Rohrbaugh and Nate Bruggeman, "Reducing Transaction Costs at North America's Borders," Belfer Center for Science and International Affairs, Harvard Kennedy School, March 20, 2018; https://www.belfercenter.org/publication/reducing-transaction-costs-north-americas-borders

staffed almost exclusively with men from poor countries—a third of all seafarers are Filipino and 98 percent are men.[15] The work is dangerous: around two thousand seafarers die each year and at any given point hundreds are held hostage by pirates who have hijacked ships and are engaged in negotiations with owners that can last years.[16]

The vulnerabilities in this system are significant. Ship crews have no interest in what they are carrying and no real ability to be curious: with about 18 inches between container stacks they could not safely access most of the cargo on the ship while at sea.[17] The level of human trafficking in cargo containers is essentially unknown. It generally receives attention when there is some kind of disaster, as when 58 Chinese immigrants were found suffocated in a container that arrived in the United Kingdom in 2000.[18] Counterfeit goods move as easily because the manifests that are supposed to itemize everything in containers are unreliable. For example, after the ship *MSC Napoli* wrecked in 2007 authorities found that 20 percent of the manifest was simply wrong.[19]

The possibility of terrorists exploiting this system to move a weapon of mass destruction into the United States has been recognized for years. Even if detected upon arrival at the port, a dirty bomb or nuclear weapon would already be in a major urban area and a vital logistical center. In a particularly alarming demonstration, ABC News successfully shipped depleted uranium through the Port of Los Angeles, the largest in the United States, in 2003.[20] Al Qaeda recruited a maritime expert in 2004 for the purpose of planning attacks using the international shipping system, and an al Qaeda operative was actually smuggled in a shipping container in 2001.[21] Nuclear bomb-making equipment has been smuggled in cargo containers: in 2003 a ship traveling from Malaysia to Libya was stopped and containers labeled "Used Machinery" were found to be filled with components for uranium centrifuges being sold by the A. Q. Khan network to Libya's Muammar al-Gadhafi.[22] North Korea operates 242 vessels, and has used them to smuggle conventional weapons.[23] It has an established smuggling network in place that could be used for proliferation.

After DHS was formed new requirements were established for information from seaborne cargo. Manifests, which contain information on both the type of cargo in a container and its physical weight and size, have to go to CBP before a container can be loaded into a cargo ship, and additional data elements referred to as "10 + 2" (10 elements of information about the importer and two about the shipper) must also be submitted.

CBP can then use this information to make a security assessment about the different entities involved in a shipment to the United States. This allows officers to identify discrepancies in information. As an example, they might note that an address or phone number used by an importer matched one previously found on cargo in which narcotics or other contraband were identified, which would allow them to single out the shipment for further inspection.

In response to these threats, in 2005 Congress passed the SAFE Port Act, which mandated that 100 percent of containers departing foreign ports for the United States had to be scanned through nonintrusive inspection equipment (basically X-ray-type machines) before boarding. Because the law did not consider how this would be implemented, very little progress has been made on this mandate and presently less than a few percent of the cargo that enters the United States is scanned. CBP has developed programs to inspect containers abroad before they can leave for the United States, through what are called the Container Security Initiative and the Secure Freight Initiative, which allow CBP officers to request inspections in foreign ports and in some instances view scanning images from those ports. While these programs have obvious security benefits, their success has been limited by their costs and the difficulty of coordinating processes at the hundreds of foreign ports where cargo departs for the United Sates. It will never be feasible to put American officers in every port around the world doing inspections. The goal should be raise standards to a level at which weapons of mass destruction moving through any part of the global supply chain would be identified and stopped.

Additionally, at the cost of hundreds of millions of dollars, stationary radiation portal monitors have been put in every U.S. port of entry. These monitors scan every container entering the United States for radiation, and officers carrying portable radiation monitors then resolve any alerts. They would most likely not be capable, however, of detecting nuclear material that had been competently shielded with lead, a fact that is commonly known and, one would imagine, a fairly simple thing for the sort of sophisticated terrorist who would be able to procure and ship a nuclear device to the United States to ascertain. Additionally, the detectors are all located on the territory of the United States. This could plausibly make sense at the land borders, where ports of entry are generally not in urban areas (with some significant exceptions), but with seaports located in places like Los Angeles, Seattle, Miami, or Newark, it would clearly be too late to identify a threat after it had been taken off a ship. Naturally occurring radiation in items like kitty litter and bananas set off frequent false alarms. Following up on a seemingly endless stream of false alarms both wastes an extraordinary amount of officer time and deadens officers to the possibility of an actual nuclear or radiological threat.

Solutions to the problems of container security have been held back by several important factors. These include the following:

- The lack of an incentive for the private sector to invest because of unclear benefits. A port will be unwilling to establish new security requirements and pass on the costs to its customers if their competitors are not doing the same and it isn't clear that there will be any specific benefit to them through the additional steps.
- The major problems of coordination among the different entities involved in international supply chains. So many stakeholders are involved in moving goods and could have to change their business processes in a new regime that there is no clear entity to coordinate an overall approach to security, and the losers from any new requirements will be more directly affected than those who benefit from an overall smoother process.
- The "is Congress just going to change the law again and introduce new requirements?" question. This overhangs most potential private investments in increased security, since a port operator is not going to want to make expensive improvements if they won't end up meeting requirements put in place by the U.S. Congress.

The land border is a particularly challenging environment for container security, because of the ongoing opportunities for contraband to be introduced or for someone to tamper with a shipment. This is especially true on the Southwest border, where, even if a shipment was perfectly safe when it left a factory, after sitting in traffic for several hours in a city like Nuevo Laredo waiting to cross, it must be reinspected. The land border is, however, the location where a true container security solution would have the most dramatic benefit, since goods do not need to be unloaded at the port of entry (as they do from planes and ships), and secure traffic could bypass congested lines at the border entirely, which would both ensure that they cross quickly and dramatically speed the overall throughput at the border.

| The evolution of the risk management regime described in the last two chapters has significant implications for the way other twenty-first-century threats will need to be addressed. Here are the essential features of this approach:

- Technological solutions that avoid major changes to new processes;
- Efforts by government to preserve the benefit of technological changes;
- Extensive information sharing within the government and between federal agencies and the private sector;
- A constant and sometimes unsuccessful struggle to balance personal privacy and security; and
- Close engagement with industry to develop regulatory regimes that meet security requirements but are tolerable for businesses.

7 | Migration and Border Security

As the processes to secure trade and travel have evolved, the challenge of managing migration and security at the land border has also changed dramatically. When people say "border security," they are generally referring to interdiction at the physical border between the ports of entry (where all crossing is illegal). Crossings between the ports are the most visible violations of law and sovereignty at the border and provoke the most visceral public response, and have therefore historically been the focus of legislation intending to crack down on security at the border. This chapter will explain the unusual twentieth-century migration challenges of the United States and the process of building our current enforcement infrastructure, and how this is being challenged by fundamental changes in the type of migration that is now occurring. It will also describe some of the structural and legal shifts that will need to occur to address the problems that exist today. The central point is that the current approach to migration and border security is based on a fundamentally twentieth-century, nation-state approach, and this is increasingly poorly suited for the larger movements of asylum seekers and long-term economic migrants from around the world that characterize market-state migration.

The Unusual Border Security Situation of the United States

In the United States, nearly all uncontrolled migration has historically come from Mexico across the Southwest border. As a result of this, twentieth-century border management in the United States was characterized by ongoing political flare-ups in both the United States and in Mexico, little cooperation between authorities binationally, an increasing emphasis on stopping migrants after they crossed or while they were crossing, and little consideration for how consequences were applied to people who were apprehended or how enforcement priorities connected to the subsequent processing of migrants after they had been stopped by the Border Patrol.

The United States is in a fairly unique situation in that over the last century the world's largest economy has shared a nearly 2,000 mile land border with a developing country, half of whose territory the United States seized by force. Large numbers of seasonal workers from Mexico moved back and forth across the border quite openly throughout the twentieth century. This makes immigration control and border security efforts much more visible, and situates any enforcement efforts in a heated political context that is different from other wealthy countries. If the United Kingdom or France want to reduce immigration from their former colonies in Pakistan or Algeria, they can simply refuse visas and deny intending migrants the ability to get on a plane. The United States has interacted with intending migrants after they arrive on its territory.

At the same time, the existing system in the United States is essentially structured to be abused by employers and to take advantage of migrants. Certain industries in the United States, in particular construction, agriculture, restaurants, hotels, landscaping, childcare, and housekeeping, simply rely on large flows of undocumented labor in order to operate at current market rates. The number of unskilled workers allowed to migrate lawfully to the United States is set far too low to meet the needs of these industries, which both draws migrants to come to the United States to work illegally and results in tacit social acceptance of this system. To a large extent, this unskilled, low-cost labor has propped up the American standard of living by making services and goods, in particular food, less expensive than they would be in other comparably wealthy countries.[1] There are also few sanctions against employers, largely because of a high standard that requires ICE to prove that they knowingly hired ineligible workers.

This unofficial but broadly accepted guest worker program puts all of the enforcement risk on the individual migrants. As a result, there are large groups of migrants who have been put in a particularly cruel legal situation. The most visible of these are the Dreamers, who were brought into the United States illegally as children, have lived here continuously, have demonstrated good moral character, and have graduated from high school or entered college. They are so-called because they would have been provided a legal status through the Development, Relief, and Education for Alien Minors (DREAM) Act, which was first introduced in 2001 by Senators Dick Durbin and Orrin Hatch. It was voted on in the Senate in 2007 and received a majority 52–44 vote but was stopped by a Republican filibuster, and passed the House in 2010 but was never subsequently brought to the floor in the Senate.

This unofficial and illicit guest worker program has been politically volatile, particularly because it pushes large numbers of people to physically cross the land border, which creates tension in border states. The border and illegal immigration have long had major political impacts in both the United States and Mexico. There have been a number of examples of state-level legislation passed in America in response to illicit flows of migrants, despite immigration enforcement having always been a federal function. In 1994 Californians passed Proposition 187, a ballot initiative designed to deny state benefits to illegal migrants and to require that any illegal migrants who did apply for social benefits were reported to federal migration authorities. While it was overturned by a U.S. district judge in 1999, it exemplifies the kind of popular backlash that can occur when immigration is perceived to be inadequately controlled. Arizona's Senate Bill 1070 in 2010 made it a state misdemeanor for a migrant to be in Arizona without carrying required documents, and imposed penalties on anyone sheltering, hiring, or transporting unregistered aliens.

Building the Modern Border Patrol

The most significant shift in enforcement at the physical border between the ports of entry began in 1992 in El Paso and then San Diego, through Operations Hold the Line and Gatekeeper, respectively. Before this point, Border Patrol agents largely focused on apprehending migrants within the United States after they had crossed the border, at locations such as transportation hubs in border cities. This was a reasonable approach given the resources, as enormous numbers of people crossed illegally and the Border Patrol's resources were extremely limited compared to the volumes they were attempting to apprehend. When Border Patrol agents were deployed to the actual border, however, illegal crossings began to drop significantly, and these operations became a model that was replicated across the border.

Before this point, the problems of lawlessness at the border were dramatic. Illegal crossings occurred with near impunity, resulting in the aforementioned backlash in places like California that felt overrun with illegal crossers. Crime and lawlessness at the border were high as guides and drug smugglers interacted with economic migrants and opportunities for exploitation were constant. Videos and photos from that time are shocking to people familiar with today's border, as there were limited physical barriers to illegal entry and masses of unidentified people would run into the United States and disperse.

Beginning in the Clinton administration, and continuing through the present day, enormous investments in border security have dramatically changed migration flows. The Border Patrol increased from around 3,000 agents in the early 1990s to over 21,000 today, with 18,000 of those deployed on the Southwest border. At this point, the number of agents is as high as it can get without a significant reduction in hiring standards—the Border Patrol has a congressionally mandated staffing floor that it has enormous trouble meeting due to the lengthy hiring process and attrition. Sensors, surveillance systems mounted on towers and vehicles, reconnaissance by aircraft and drones, 700 miles of fences and vehicle barriers, and vastly expanded transportation resources for border patrol agents have all made it much more difficult to illegally cross the border.

The Border Patrol has evolved from an organization charged with bringing order to a lawless situation and stopping out of control illegal crossings into one with much broader capabilities that responds increasingly to human smuggling and trafficking, drug smuggling, and other activities driven by organized crime. Crossing illegally is now a fundamentally more difficult proposition than it was even several years ago, and traffic between the ports is now focused on remote areas and nearly always requires knowledgeable and expensive guides. Here are the essential elements of this approach:

- Forward deployments of agents to deter illegal crossings of the physical border.
- Expanded infrastructure, which can include fences to create physical barriers in urban or other high-traffic areas, vehicle barriers where a car or truck could attempt to drive across, and access roads that allow Border Patrol agents to patrol close to the border and to "cut sign" (where agents drag an implement behind their

vehicle that smooths the road and allows them to identify footprints when they return).

- Surveillance and detection technology, including fixed towers, aerostats (basically large tethered balloons with sensors), cameras, sensors, vehicle mounted systems, systems that can be carried by agents, and support from helicopters, planes, and drones that can identify illicit crossers.

- Staffing increases and temporary deployments to high-traffic areas—the Border Patrol has developed a cadre of highly trained officers known as BORSTAR (for Border Patrol Search, Trauma, and Rescue) and BORTAC (for Border Patrol Tactical Unit) who can be moved quickly to high-risk areas to perform interdictions or rescues of migrants in distress.

- Intelligence about when and where cartels and human smuggling organizations are staging and preparing to cross.

- Expanded cross-border partnership through close engagement with counterparts across the border, which for the United States means Mexico and Canada. Despite the rhetoric of the Trump administration, the partnership between Mexican and American law enforcement at the border has steadily improved in recent decades, and Mexican authorities are the only officers who can break up cartel staging areas for smuggling operations.

- Countering other smuggling innovations—ultralight aircraft, submersibles, panga-type boats, catapults, and more. As it becomes more difficult to smuggle people and goods, criminal organizations have turned to increasingly innovative smuggling methods. Single-person ultralight aircraft have been used frequently to smuggle drugs—pilots may or may not have had any training but are pointed in the right direction and sent across the border with the expectation that even if they crash the drugs can likely be recovered.

- Considered application of consequences to illicit crossers to ensure that the most onerous administrative or criminal processes are targeted at crossers who pose the greatest threat. The Border Patrol began doing this in 2010 through the Consequence Delivery System, which provided officers with a guide to which sorts of apprehended individuals should be quickly voluntarily returned (such as a mother with a young child) and which should be recommended for prosecution (e.g., a 17-year-old cartel guide who has been apprehended a dozen times before). This was abandoned by the Trump administration when it began its immoral and ineffective "zero tolerance" policy of recommending every adult border crosser for prosecution, with the intention of using family separations as a punishment to deter additional migrants.

This is exemplified by the work that was done to bring the Tucson Sector under control during the Obama administration. In 2010, apprehensions in the Tucson Sector had continued to stay above 250,000 annually. In response to this, CBP took a series of steps that brought Arizona under control by applying the steps listed above. This began as a coordinated operations plan and developed into a fully harmonized effort where all of the CBP operations were under the control of a single commander and agents, technology, and aviation support had been redeployed to Tucson from around the country. This effort had dramatic results, and within two years the number of apprehensions annually had been halved, and crossings have continued to decline.

Another striking example of this comes from the Yuma Sector, the furthest western portion of Arizona. In 2005, as traffic was driven away from the San Diego area, there were 138,000 apprehensions and a genuinely frightening level of lawlessness, including things like hundreds of attacks on agents and trucks racing across the border (which then had no vehicle fence) and getting into high-speed pursuits on U.S. roads. In response, CBP took many of the steps described above, including adding a vehicle fence, deploying new agents, and installing advanced technology for surveillance, and in 2016 there were about 6,100 apprehensions overall.

One major ongoing challenge has been effectively dealing with tunnels. Cross-border tunnels are one of the most vexing problems of cross-border law enforcement, as a functioning tunnel can move enormous quantities of contraband, but especially narcotics. Compact, high-profit drugs like cocaine, heroin, and methamphetamine can be moved in enormous quantities through tunnels, and it has even been reported that the Sinaloa cartel is technologically capable of building tunnels so small and advanced that they can be used as pneumatic tubes—shooting packages under the border as if they were within a bank.[2]

Illegal crossings have shifted dramatically in response to these changes

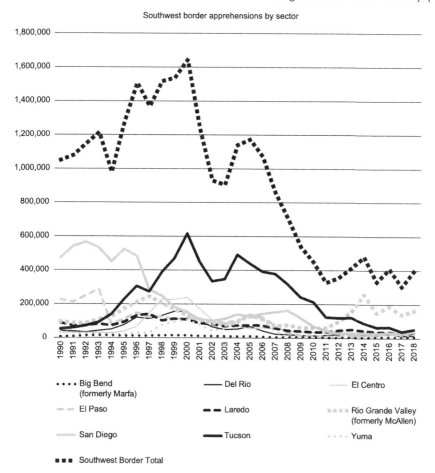

Fig. 1. Southwest border apprehensions by sector

in flows, as is shown in figure 1 with sector by sector apprehension totals.[3] These statistics show the ways that migration flows have changed since increasing amounts of resources began being devoted to border security in the early 1990s.

First, illegal flows clearly move in response to increases in enforcement. In 1992, over 70 percent of all crossings occurred in the San Diego and El Paso Sectors, where migrants could quickly disappear into urban areas on the U.S. side of the border. As the Border Patrol grew from 3,555 agents in 1992 to over 7,000 in 1997, increased numbers of agents were forward deployed on the line, and as physical barriers to crossing were constructed, crossings in El Paso and San Diego dropped and have remained at much lower levels since then. Flows then shifted from San Diego inland to the El Centro Sector, covering California's Imperial Valley, and then on to Yuma, in western Arizona. In Texas, they moved from El Paso east to Laredo and the Rio Grande Valley. In response, in the late 1990s and early 2000s a series of operations were conducted to increase the deployments of agents and technology to new areas. Operation Rio Grande, beginning in 1998, pushed traffic west into the more remote Del Rio Sector, and Operation Jump Start in Yuma in the early 2000s caused the bulk of the remaining traffic to move to the remote Tucson Sector. A major effort beginning in 2010 that involved increases in both agents and technology and the establishment of a single commander with control over all of CBP's assets in the region led to dramatic reductions in crossings in Tucson in recent years.

Second, flows overall have dropped enormously, from around a million and a half apprehensions every year in the 1990s to between 300,000 and 500,000 in recent years. The one exception to this has been the increase in Central Americans arriving in the Rio Grande Valley, but this is a fundamentally different kind of traffic, and this increase actually obscures the fact that Mexican migration has continued to drop steadily. In 2016, 218,110 of the apprehensions on the Southwest border were of non-Mexicans, with 140,496 of those occurring in the Rio Grande Valley. This means that only 190,760 of the apprehensions on the entire Southwest border were of Mexican migrants. The change is even more dramatic in specific high-traffic locations like El Paso, where they have averaged about 10,000 apprehensions a year from 2012 to 2017, while in the 1990s the numbers were consistently at least 10 times as high. As will be discussed in more detail below, these Central American migrants are arriving specifically because of the protections that they are afforded under current law, and are actively seeking out Border Patrol agents to turn themselves in to. The bipartisan goal of the build-up in border security resources that began in the Clinton administration and continued under Bush and Obama was to end the lawlessness at the border and uncontrolled crossing by Mexican nationals. The Border Patrol has, by any reasonable standard, been extremely effective at accomplishing this, and the number of Mexican apprehensions has now been reduced by over 88 percent from what it was in 2000.

Apprehending people crossing the border illegally is always accompanied by a process to return individuals to their home country. One of the most volatile and difficult aspects of border security is the detention and removal of illegal migrants, especially those who have committed crimes after arriving in the United States. There are a few fundamental constraints that shape the way this works in the United States. First, normally ICE has the funding and capacity to detain about 34,000 adult individuals. The Trump administration has consistently increased the number of people in detention to above 50,000, which is a major increase but still fewer than the number of people who are being apprehended crossing the border in some months.[4] The space to detain families is much more limited, and ICE does not detain unaccompanied children, who are held by Health and Human Services until they can be placed with a sponsor. Additionally, ICE has country-by-country agreements to allow repatriation and has to work with consulates to obtain travel documents for anyone who will be removed, and many countries either put administrative limits on the volume who can be returned (like El Salvador), or refuse to recognize migrants as their nationals (China often does this). Because of these limits on capacity, at any given point ICE has to make a decision about who it keeps in detention and prioritizes for immediate removal, and who must be released. There are also judicially imposed limits on how long ICE can keep someone in detention without beginning removal proceedings. It is important to note that some of ICE's releases of criminal aliens are discretionary but many are not, a distinction that is generally ignored by the agency's critics.

Prior to the Obama administration, ICE has dealt with this by focusing its efforts on criminals who have been detained by local law enforcement and can be transferred into ICE custody. The difference with the Obama administration's approach, and part of the reason for the controversy around the executive actions, is that the Obama administration made the decision to make these prioritizations explicit in guidance from the homeland security secretary. In 2010 the director of ICE, John T. Morton, issued a memorandum that directed the use of this law enforcement discretion to focus resources on criminal migrants. Finding criminal migrants who have disappeared into communities and who are not apprehended by state or local law enforcement is extremely difficult for ICE, and as a result of this guidance the overall numbers of criminal migrants removed dropped significantly, although a higher percentage of those removed were the types of violent criminals that most people agree need to be prioritized.

The result of this system is that deportation in the United States is used as a deterrent rather than a consistently applied consequence for entering illegally. Removals will be done in a largely capricious and opportunistic way, because the organization conducting these efforts is under-resourced and doing an extremely unpleasant job. Removable individuals come to the attention of ICE when they interact with authorities, which results in stories about migrants who have been in the United States for years removed after being pulled over for having a busted taillight. As a result the experience of migrants under the current system will always be arbitrary.

Changes in Southwest Border Migration

As the Border Patrol became more and more effective at interdicting people crossing between the ports of entry, a strange thing started to happen. Increasing numbers of migrants started crossing the border and turning themselves in to Border Patrol agents. Unlike previous crossers who would attempt to evade Border Patrol agents, the vulnerable populations of unaccompanied children and family groups that arrived were actually searching for agents to give themselves up. These migrants were seeking specific legal protections and would claim them after being apprehended. Instead of being able to deal with asylum claimants internationally, the United States now was processing hundreds of thousands of people who were already on U.S. territory.

Many of them had legitimate claims to asylum based on the extremely violent and gang-controlled conditions in Central America, and those whose claims were denied would be in the United States for years during the immigration court process, with ample opportunities to disappear. Border security was previously a problem of lawlessness and evading interdiction, and became a complex refugee processing and human smuggling problem, with migrants spending thousands of dollars on guides to cross the river and often many times more than that to arrive at the Southwest border.

This shift in the type of migration had enormous effects on the administrative complications in processing an apprehended migrant. As an example, an adult Mexican who is caught crossing illegally by the Border Patrol can be removed very quickly, especially when migrants agree to be voluntarily returned, and in many cases the Border Patrol will be the only government entity that a migrant will interact with before being returned to Mexico's migration agency. When a Central American child crosses between the ports, however, the process is much more complicated. First, the Border Patrol will do initial in-processing and screening at the border patrol stations. The Border Patrol must then transfer the minor into the custody of Health and Human Services' Office of Refugees and Resettlement, who will then likely spend at least a month working to place the minor with family members or in a foster home as the legal process begins. The minor will then begin his or her hearings at immigration court, which is run by the Department of Justice's Executive Office of Immigration Review. Cases can take several years with lengthy appeals processes (children are not legally required to have counsel but the Obama administration made it a priority to increase representation for unaccompanied minors, either by direct funding or by recruiting pro bono representation). At this point, if a minor is ordered removed, ICE will effect the removal. If a minor does not willingly comply with the removal order or they are not able to be found, ICE will have to send a fugitive operations team to attempt to track down the minor based on their previous addresses and other information. One a minor is removed, the State Department works with the governments of Guatemala, Honduras, and El Salvador to fund and expand reintegration programs so that children do not end up immediately back in dangerous situations. This is an extremely complex, multiyear process that is very difficult to coordinate across the multiple government agencies involved, and the administrative burden created by this type of migration is completely different from what was caused by historic migration patterns.

When the type of migration at the border began to change in 2013 the result was to quickly overwhelm existing systems during the Obama administration. This was dramatically shown in the summer of 2014, when suddenly the largest bottleneck was processing migrants once they had turned themselves in to officers or agents. The central challenge was that the government had to figure out how to process a population that required special protections in a volume that had never been seen before. As anyone who saw the pictures from that summer knows, Border Patrol stations just were not built with the expectation that they would be used to house children or families. Health and Human Services also had inadequate housing capacity, and quickly was desperately looking for additional space. In response, the Obama administration turned to the Mexican government, which quickly increased its enforcement efforts and was soon doubling the number of Central American migrants it was deporting while they attempted to transit Mexico.[5]

The numbers of migrants dropped at the beginning of the Trump administration, as the president's campaign language left many migrants expecting a crackdown, and Fiscal Year 2017 had the lowest total apprehensions in modern history. The drop did not last, however, and the numbers quickly began to increase in 2018. Despite the Trump administration's willingness to be appallingly cruel to migrants, most infamously through separating families as part of a disastrous "zero tolerance" policy, the numbers of people arriving continued to increase dramatically in 2019. Border Patrol apprehensions spiked to nearly 93,000 in March, climbing to 99,000 in April and then to over 132,000 in May, completely overwhelming the resources at the border.[6] Most of the asylum seekers continued to arrive between the ports of entry; upon encountering the Border Patrol, record numbers of families would turn themselves in. There is nothing remotely like an appropriate system to safely intake and process these vulnerable populations at the Southwest border. The Border Patrol lacked the manpower and resources to process, house, feed, and otherwise care for the flood of migrants. The media quickly captured images of migrants being housed in makeshift camps under El Paso highways. Story after story recounted migrants being housed in cramped, overcapacity temporary holding cells at Border Patrol stations. U.S. Citizenship and Immigration Services immigration officers could not keep up with the number of claims. Incredibly, a president who had centered his campaign on border security had presided in 2019 over the largest sustained increase in illegal entry into the United States in decades. The apprehension numbers only began to go down after the administration switched tactics and compelled the Mexican government to ramp up its enforcement efforts under the threat of tariffs, and the Trump administration began to force migrants to wait for processing in extremely dangerous Mexican border cities.

Market-State Migration

The shift in the nature of migration at the Southwest border tracks to the nation-state to market-state transition. As the state increasingly bases its legitimacy in providing the greatest possible individual opportunity rather than the well-being of a cohesive social or ethnic group, the politics of migration and the type of migration that occurs changes.

Refugees and asylum seekers used to be something that largely happened in other countries, the United States could deal with it as a foreign policy problem, and the existing approach to refugees and asylum seekers was based on them staying where they are. Migrants increasingly won't just be from adjacent countries or places with long-standing connections. Market-state migration is also much more organized than it was before, as migrants have sophisticated understandings of the legal framework in the target country, extensive communication networks, and are making a major investment to make the trip.

Market-states are by nature more ethnically diverse and better at integrating immigrants. Arguments against migration in a nation-state context focus on security, ethnicity, economic costs, and cultural affinity. For much of the twentieth century the United States had huge restrictions on nonwhite immigration, most notably through the Chinese Exclusion Act, which remained in effect until 1943, and the Immigration Act of 1924, which aggressively favored migrants from Northern European countries to the exclusion of nearly everywhere else.[7] In the modern United States cultural affinity is much less relevant, ethnicity is offensive, and the elite consensus is that migration provides economic benefits, so people who want to restrict immigration focus on security arguments.

In a market-state, migration limits seem much more arbitrary. If anyone can be given the opportunity to succeed and there are essentially unlimited numbers of people who would like to migrate to developed market-states if they had the opportunity, then it is much less obvious who exactly should benefit from that opportunity and how the limits should be drawn.

Effectively responding to this new situation will require new immigration laws. The legal framework for immigration in the United States is objectionable to basically everyone. There generally has been a centrist elite consensus in the United States about the necessity of comprehensive immigration reform along the lines of the bill that passed the Senate in 2013. This approach focused on increased enforcement resources, establishing a guest worker program that would allow much higher levels of unskilled workers to enter the United States temporarily, increased worksite enforcement of immigration laws (currently employers face almost no meaningful sanction for hiring ineligible workers), and providing a path to citizenship for people who are currently in the United States illegally.[8] Much of this would be an improvement. The emphasis on worksite enforcement would be a better use of law enforcement resources, to the extent that it shifts the sanctions from migrants to the employers who hire them. A path to citizenship is also desperately overdue: people who have been living in the United States for years must be given the opportunity to obtain legal status. A guest worker program would provide a legal basis for unskilled migration, which would be an improvement over the existing unofficial system. It is not clear, however, that it is desirable to have a permanent underclass of foreign workers in the United States. If the American economy needs foreign workers we should be prepared to provide them legal status and a clear path to citizenship.

This kind of immigration reform would improve the existing system, but it is largely structured to address the migration problems of the twentieth century and remove the most egregious unfairness of the existing system. To effectively address twenty-first-century migration, there are two major changes that need to be made to the U.S. approach:

First, legal immigration should be increased and there should be a major increase in admissions based on humanitarian criteria.

The number of immigrants allowed into the United States should be increased significantly through a major expansion of the humanitarian categories. In a market-state any restrictions on migration are going to seem arbitrary, so the best approach is to make our decisions as ethical as possible—pick a large number of people who are most in need around the world and work seriously to integrate them into our society.

America's existing humanitarian protections are based on protecting people who are persecuted by governments because they are members of a societal group. Current law does not provide protections for people who are victimized by nonstate actors. It also does not apply to dire economic conditions: a person who is fleeing the Guatemalan highlands with their family because a coffee harvest has failed and they and their children will starve if they stay is not a candidate for asylum under existing law. The United States could expand these categories to allow a defined number of extremely needy people around the world to migrate for economic reasons. The existing system also has country-specific caps on the immigrants that disproportionately affect countries like Mexico, India, China, and the

Philippines that make the common "get in line" refrain ridiculous—for people from those countries the line is decades longer than for those from elsewhere.[9] Expanding the categories for humanitarian protections, significantly increasing the number of people admitted, and reducing the distortions caused by country caps would provide an ethical basis for a twenty-first-century immigration system. This number should also be defined by capacity: migrants need places to stay, food, schools for their children, the legal right to work, and probably assistance while they adapt. It is irresponsible to just assume that informal networks or charity organizations will figure everything out. This would also provide a defensible explanation for who the United States does not let in, which the current system lacks.

Expanding humanitarian migration would also have major indirect benefits. First, it would provide a direct way to assist desperate civilians around the world who would otherwise be forced to turn to criminal smuggling organizations. Second, it would be one of the best possible ways to demonstrate the values of the United States internationally and to counter the propaganda of terrorist groups.

The "merit-based" approach associated with members of the Trump administration such as Jared Kushner, which would favor people with advanced degrees or special talents beyond the existing employment visas, is deeply misguided. The social benefits of migration are unpredictable—coming to the United States to study, fathering a child, and then leaving the child is a pretty undesirable behavior, but it's what the fathers of Steve Jobs and Barack Obama did. There is also no need to further tilt the immigration system to benefit the rich, which is a major indirect result of any merit system (the people who can obtain doctorates or coding skills have the time and resources to do so). Wealthy people are always going to have the resources to benefit from migration; there's no need to further stack the deck.

Second, the primary location for refugee intake cannot be the Southwest border.

The Southwest border is not an appropriate place to intake large numbers of people seeking humanitarian protections. There cannot be one category of laws for people who arrive at the Southwest border and another category for everyone else, including desperate people coming to embassies or consulates around the world. By perpetuating a process where people who can physically travel to the United States have different protections, we create incentives for migrants to take a dangerous journey and encourage human smuggling networks, while providing no assistance for the most vulnerable people who lack the thousands of dollars necessary to travel to the border.

The Southwest border is an awful place to process asylum seekers. The cities on the Mexican side are some of the most dangerous in the world. The American ports of entry were designed to quickly process people and conveyances and have totally inadequate facilities to conduct detailed credible fear interviews. Huge influxes of people with no places to stay will overwhelm existing systems if the migrants themselves have to arrange shelter, particularly in transit countries. They will also be subject to abuse and exploitation. Expanding the humanitarian categories for legal immigration would provide a genuine legal pathway for desperate people from places like Central America to come to the United States.

Effective interdiction at the Southwest border will absolutely need to be maintained. Interdicting illegal crossing is an important component of a twenty-first-century migration regime, because officials have to be able to identify who is entering the country. American officials need to know who is entering the country and be able to stop people who are potentially dangerous, and this will require an effective interdiction regime at the Southwest border.

This will mean there will be people who need to be removed. There is nothing reactionary about believing that the United States should be able to actively decide how many migrants to accept and what criteria they should meet, and that people who are apprehended illegally entering the country or overstaying their visas should be removed.

There would still be a certain number of people who arrive at the Southwest border seeking asylum, and they need to be able to make their case while being kept safe through a genuine internationally coordinated program to keep them in a secure location. A regional approach could establish safe locations with direct access to American officials for expedited hearings throughout Mexico and Central America, which would ensure that the migrants who are actually fleeing imminent violence are protected. This would be in stark contrast to the Trump administration's program of having migrants remain in Mexico while they wait to eventually be processed at U.S. ports of entry, which both ensures that the migrants will be unsafe and subject to abuse and that the Mexican cities will be overwhelmed. The ridiculously named "safe third country agreements" to return asylum seekers to Honduras or El Salvador, consistently some of the world's most dangerous and gang-run countries, are even more disgraceful.

8 | Putting Off the Evil Day

The discussion of migration has demonstrated how a structure designed for twentieth-century challenges can quickly be overwhelmed when the strategic context changes. There are three additional areas where the U.S. government is particularly misaligned with emergent threats, which has been demonstrated by increasing problems effectively responding to new situations. In each of these areas there will need to be the kind of restructuring that are taking place in the area of passenger vetting and border management in order to adapt to the new security environment. These exemplify the ways that national security threats now have direct domestic effects, and the mismatches between our existing institutions and the challenges of nonstate transnational actors.

Cybersecurity

Officials have been warning of an impending cybersecurity disaster for decades. The U.S. government approach to cybersecurity, however, is fundamentally focused and resourced for military and intelligence operations against foreign countries and law enforcement investigations of cyber crime. This is a disastrously mismatched approach to the most transnational and decentralized threat imaginable.

In 1996, Deputy Attorney General Jaime Gorelick warned of an impending "cyber Pearl Harbor,"[1] and the alarming statements have just escalated. Since there has not been a cyber attack causing damage and loss of life on the scale of Pearl Harbor or 9/11 in the intervening decades, it is easy to dismiss these warnings. Cyber vulnerabilities are not static, however, and are continuously growing as more and more of modern life is conducted over digital networks and more and more sensitive data is collected electronically. When Gorelick warned about cyber attacks, people didn't carry phones that recorded everywhere they moved and all of their personal, professional, and commercial interactions. Facebook didn't exist, you couldn't deposit a check electronically, and cars didn't rely on software to operate their braking and acceleration. The fact that widely identified vulnerabilities have not yet been exploited should provide little comfort, as it can take quite a bit of time before something is possible and actually done. The spy novelist Charles McCarry wrote a book that involved terrorists hijacking airplanes and crashing them into American targets in 1979.[2]

There are three things making the problem worse and worse. The first is the increasing amount of extremely sensitive information kept on government networks at the federal, state, and local level. The second is the even more sensitive information that is being gathered by private industry. The third is the lack of resilience and redundancy in digital networks. As these threats have grown, the government's response to cybersecurity has been consistently ineffective and shows clearly how an outdated strategy can leave problems unaddressed until an active crisis.

Government Networks

The U.S. government, by the very nature of the activities it conducts, collects an enormous amount of potentially sensitive information. The slow and difficult process of automating this information collection has accelerated in recent decades, so that paper files have been largely digitized and new information is collected in electronic form. From investigative case files to cargo manifest details to medical information, all of this is now stored electronically on government systems. The U.S. government has repeatedly failed to protect electronically stored sensitive information about American citizens. As a federal employee it is easy to be numb to the constant notifications that the most private information you have entrusted to the government has repeatedly been breached, but that should not obscure the scale of what has happened and how much sensitive information has been infiltrated.

Most significantly, the Standard Form 86 security screening data for federal employees held by the Office of Personnel Management was breached in 2015 by hackers who were reported to be affiliated with the Chinese government.[3] The fact that this was caused by garden-variety incompetence as opposed to a *Mission Impossible*–style infiltration by foreign agents did not limit how much damage was done. The Chinese government has been provided with a straightforward way to identify every covert employee of the United States government.

This information is about as sensitive as you can imagine, and has to include any information about financial problems, personal issues, substance use, psychological information, detailed information about foreign friends and contacts, address and foreign travel data, and basically anything else that could make you unfit to handle sensitive information, which has to be certified to be accurate under pain of criminal penalties. It is then supplemented by a series of interviews done by investigators who go to every address you list and talk individually to every contact you disclose. People they interview are also under oath, and are asked in detail about the most potentially incriminating activities and aspects of your life, and their interviews are kept as part of your file and used to determine whether you merit a clearance. Incredibly and outrageously, the Office of Personnel Management failed to take even minimal safeguards to protect this information and kept it on out of date computers that were thoroughly compromised by hackers in 2015, who stole this information for over 21.5 *million* individuals, including military personnel, as well as 5.6 million sets of fingerprints.

The amount of deeply sensitive personal information that was accessed is staggering. It is literally as if I and everyone else who had access to sensitive information had applied for a security clearance with Chinese intelligence, submitted to interrogation by them about my family, friends, and lifestyle under penalty of perjury, and willingly let them interview all of my acquaintances and neighbors for the past decade (twice in my case). The constant drumbeat of news about cyber leaks can deaden people to the actual consequences, but this kind of abject incompetence and irresponsibility is the sort of thing that can have incredibly negative and possibly fatal consequences for national security personnel and other public servants.

Private Sector Data Collection

Sensitive information held by private companies has been shown to be equally insecure. It is just as easy to become numbed to the frequent reports about breaches of customer data, but a few events highlight the scale of the negligence and the inadequacy of existing protections on consumer information.

In 2017 Equifax, one three major American credit monitoring companies, was infiltrated and hackers stole personal information for over 145 million Americans that included Social Security numbers, driver's license numbers and additional information, tax identification numbers, and credit card numbers.[4] Because of the nature of the monitoring that Equifax conducts, this included literally all of the information that would be necessary to steal a consumer's identify and open fraudulent financial accounts. The breach is particularly galling because most of the people whose data was compromised did not know what they were providing to Equifax; it was done by third-party companies who extend credit to consumers.

This is all the more concerning because companies are now collecting much larger amounts of personal data about Americans than has ever been available in the past. There are companies with extremely effective internal cybersecurity practices that are still creating enormous vulnerabilities because of the information they collect for commercial purposes. There are multiple companies that now track information as sensitive as every place a person goes, all of their personal and professional communications, full biometric identities of their faces and fingers, the layout and shape of their homes, every conversation conducted in a home, the food and beverages someone buys, physical activity and sleep patterns, and more. Even if their purposes are entirely benign, the scale of the personal information being collected raises major security and privacy concerns. Also, given that no security system is infallible, the simple collection of this information by companies is cause for concern.

There is a long list of examples. Apple is now collecting full facial biometrics through its Face ID feature, which makes it easier to unlock your phone and use certain features in exchange for voluntarily giving the company a biometric identity that is vastly superior and more detailed than anything kept by the government. This is in addition to the existing fingerprint identification that the company collects through Touch ID.[5] Amazon now has a feature that controls access to customers' homes and allows couriers to enter to deliver packages.[6] Roomba, which makes autonomous robotic vacuums, was reported to be mapping customers' homes and selling the information collected by their products.[7] The personal nature of the information collected by Uber was dramatically shown when a former employee declared in court that Uber employees freely tracked the movements of politicians, celebrities, and exes.[8] Google has gone from targeting advertisements to customers based on the content of their emails to actually suggesting the replies.[9] Facebook is perhaps the most dramatic example. The company essentially surveils its users and analyzes their activities, including all of their personal relationships and tracking where they physically go and who they interact with through their phones. This private company is conducting surveillance of market-state citizens at a scale beyond anything that has previously existed, or could have existed.[10]

The privacy concerns about all of this are obvious, but in addition to questions about how the companies are handling this information, another question needs to be considered: What happens if a hostile actor were to gain access to this information? Especially when company after company suffers data breaches, it is necessary to take a hard look at whether these companies could all perpetually prevent a determined cyber attack backed by the government of a hostile foreign power from accessing this information.

The Government's Failure to Organize Itself for Cyber Threats

Given this situation, one might expect that the federal government had taken decisive steps to meet these threats. It has not. Responsibility for cybersecurity is dispersed across a number of different departments and agencies, many of which are feuding over bureaucratic territory. Astonishingly, the key roles and responsibilities within the federal government for response to a cyber incident weren't even defined until Presidential Policy Directive 41 was issued on July 26, *2016*.[11] The law enforcement, intelligence, and military responses that the U.S government has attempted to this point are a terrible match for nonstate or quasi-state cyber actors, but the government has not seriously begun to adapt.

The investigation, arrest, and prosecution on which existing law enforcement approaches rely are practically irrelevant to cyber crime. To effectively prosecute a crime by a foreign hacker requires valid and enforceable subpoenas across every relevant jurisdiction for the crime, which are impossible to obtain in a practical amount of time.[12] Hackers based in countries disinclined to cooperate with U.S. criminal enforcement, like the 12 Russian hackers indicted by Special Counsel Robert Mueller in 2018 for hacking American campaign officials,[13] are almost guaranteed to escape punishment.

The most glaring failures have been in protecting the security of unclassified and civilian systems. The primary reason for this has been that the center of gravity for the U.S. government's cyber activities has remained the NSA, which has effectively defended its bureaucratic turf, is structured for offensive operations, and is legally prohibited from addressing vulnerabilities to civilian systems. Despite the NSA's role as an intelligence agency, its approach to cybersecurity has always been militarily focused. The NSA director was historically a three-star admiral or general until Defense Secretary Robert Gates elevated the position to four stars and made it dual-hatted with the leadership of the military's U.S. Cyber Command in 2008.[14] Despite the cutting edge technical capabilities of the NSA and Cyber Command, their approach is fundamentally twentieth century: it is entirely focused on interdicting threats internationally and on operations against foreign countries.

The inadequacies of a totally offensive approach to cybersecurity have long been clear. Again and again the U.S. government has attempted to fill the gaping holes in American information security and it has been stopped by (1) the need for legal changes and (2) the primacy of Defense and the NSA and their focus on offensive cyber activities.

- One of the first efforts to organize the U.S. government on this issue was through the Computer Security Act of 1987, which put the NSA in charge of military computers and classified networks and the Commerce Department's National Bureau of Standards in charge of the rest. The National Bureau of Standards did not have the necessary technical capacity, and actually found itself at cross-purposes to NSA. When NSA analysts discovered vulnerabilities in software they wanted to keep them secret rather than fix the gap, in order to exploit the software against foreign opponents.[15]
- This emphasis on keeping gaps open in order to use the vulnerabilities against international opponents was raised to greater prominence in the late 1990s under Director Michael Hayden with the doctrine of Computer Network Exploitation, which directly focused on finding ways to enter enemy networks to be able to quickly exploit them in case of war. It also meant that American citizens and companies remained exposed to foreign governments or criminals using the same weaknesses against them.[16]
- In 2008, in response to a particularly alarming briefing about vul-

nerabilities to computer networks, President Bush signed a national security presidential directive (NSPD-54) to address vulnerabilities in civilian and government networks and Congress appropriated $17.3 billion for implementation of the plan. The plan fell apart quickly, with most of the resources going to the NSA, which used them to expand its existing activities and backed out of participating in the DHS-led Einstein 2 project to identify malicious activity on unclassified networks and provide alerts.[17]

- In 2011 Cyber Command was made responsible for the security of critical cyber infrastructure. The problem was that they had no authorities to operate on civilian networks and continued to see their primary mission as offensive and international—so the people we have given the job to can't do the job and also do not think it is their job. In response they focused on penetrating adversaries' networks in order to try to stop attacks before they could be launched while actively opposing any measures that would require them to share information with DHS.[18]

- In 2015 President Obama issued an executive order setting up information exchange sessions between the NSA and the FBI and industry, but the order went out of its way to make clear that it was not intended as meaningful regulation. It went so far as to explicitly state "nothing in this order shall be construed to provide an agency with authority to regulate critical infrastructure."[19]

Clearly, this problem requires a new approach. The cycle of NSA and Cyber Command receiving the majority of resources, and then given jobs they legally cannot do because other under-resourced parts of the government are dismissed as incompetent, needs to be broken. Resources are going to have to be redirected to address vulnerabilities instead of continuing to attempt the impossible feat of intercepting threats around the world before they materialize. Former DHS secretary Janet Napolitano has called for a committee of public and private sector experts like the 9/11 Commission that would be convened by the president and directly address the outstanding questions that have remained unresolved for years.[20] Something on this scale should be done before the forcing function of a disaster makes it unavoidable.

Organized Crime

The U.S. government, led by the FBI, was extremely effective at dealing with twentieth-century organized crime. The structures and strategies that served so well in the past, however, are very poorly matched to the market-state criminal groups that are increasingly prevalent.

In the twentieth century the work of countering criminal organizations was mostly focused on investigating, arresting, and prosecuting the leaders of the groups. As criminal organizations have become increasingly decentralized and cellular, and as the levels of violence in countries where narcotics are produced or transported to the United States have reached appalling levels (which also drives illicit migration flows), it has been made clear that arresting and extraditing the leaders of these organizations is no longer an adequate strategy. One of the most significant needs in law enforcement is to effectively apply the lessons from counterterror efforts to problems of coordination and information sharing that have long hampered coordinated work against organized crime. By treating organized crime as a homeland security threat, and applying all of the tools that have been developed in other areas, including preventing people or companies affiliated with organized crime from using travel or trade networks, establishing watch lists so that foreign, state, and local partners know when they are dealing with members of criminal organizations, and sharing information between agencies that may have collected other pieces of the puzzle, officials could much more effectively respond to the decentralized criminal networks that modern society faces.

Organized crime has been the purview of the Justice Department since the creation of the FBI and the successful work to dismantle the Mafia. Because the FBI thoroughly shifted its focus to counterterrorism after 9/11, the traditional mission of countering organized crime became much less of a priority and received fewer resources than it had previously. This is understandable, as the primary concern of any FBI director is to make sure that another 9/11-style attack does not occur on their watch. As a result of this, however, other U.S. law enforcement agencies have taken a more central role in countering organized crime:

- The Drug Enforcement Administration, which only focuses on counternarcotics;
- ICE, which has incredibly broad authorities and ends up involved

in cases as diverse as counterfeit Super Bowl merchandise and artifact smuggling;

- The Bureau of Alcohol, Tobacco, Firearms and Explosives, which focuses narrowly on the illicit firearms and explosives used by criminal organizations; and
- Numerous state, local, tribal, and international entities.

Many criminal organizations will be involved in multiple lines of criminal business, branching out from narcotics smuggling to human trafficking and smuggling, extortion, firearms trafficking, counterfeit goods, money laundering, and other illicit activities. The agencies involved are focused on different parts of the problem and have different priorities, so that no one may end up actually focused on the overall threat. This also means that criminal organizations such as the Central American Mara Salvatrucha (MS-13) and Barrio 18 gangs, which are responsible for crime within the United States and have driven much of the horrific violence and instability that has resulted in flows of hundreds of thousands of Central American children and families to the Southwest border, are treated as comparatively low priorities because they are less involved in narcotics smuggling. I vividly remember a conversation I had at the National Security Council with a colleague who worked exclusively on organized crime issues when we both realized that while we knew the names of and closely tracked the activities of even mid-level Mexican cartel leaders we had only a limited understanding of Central American gangs and couldn't name their leaders. The result of these various sources of disconnect has been ongoing coordination problems, interagency infighting, and a failure to use all of the tools and apply all of the lessons that have been learned in other areas to the threat of organized crime.

The 9/11 Commission report identifies a number of critical failures of information sharing and bureaucratic turf wars that contributed to the failure of intelligence on 9/11. Many of these have now either been addressed or significantly improved in the counterterrorism context. As an example, before 9/11, if a law enforcement officer or intelligence analyst identified some particularly notable piece of information about terrorist plans, their incentives were to keep the information from other agencies in order to develop a case. Now, any analyst knows that if an attempted attack occurs and she had relevant information that had not been shared, it would be the end of her career.

This is notably not yet the case in the world of organized crime, although a pilot program has finally begun to establish a watch list for members of transnational criminal organizations. Agencies compete to investigate the same kinds of cases and organizations and actively fight to keep from sharing information that could disrupt criminal activity but jeopardize a larger case. As an example, information about noncitizens who are known drug traffickers and cartel members identified in DEA case files may not be shared with CBP officers, who will then process and allow dangerous people to enter the country. While this may sometimes be necessary to protect confidential sources or prevent suspects from realizing that law enforcement is aware of their activities, the standard for keeping information from federal law enforcement partners is very low. The institutional bias should be toward sharing with law enforcement partners, rather than keeping information from them. Instead, an individual case agent may currently make the determination about whether investigative information can be shared.

The twenty-first-century homeland security model is fundamentally different from the criminal justice model, which creates ongoing tension between homeland security practitioners and traditional law enforcement investigators. A traditional criminal justice approach, based largely on successful work against organized crime, says "X is a criminal, and because of this he or she should be arrested and prosecuted." The homeland security model says "X is a criminal and must be denied the infrastructure and opportunity that would allow him or her to take criminal actions." The key difference is whether criminal actions should be punished, or disrupted and prevented. The focus on prevention and disruption has been taken to its logical conclusion in counterterrorism and systems are in place to prevent terrorists from taking any kind of harmful action, but it has not yet been applied effectively to transnational criminal organizations.

The success of counterterrorism efforts since 9/11 and the extremely limited negative consequences caused by the dramatic increase in the amount of information being shared throughout the intelligence and law enforcement communities shows that information sharing is nothing for federal agencies to be afraid of. The pilot program that began establishing consolidated organized crime watch lists like those that exist for known and suspected terrorists must be continued and expanded. These efforts actually result in investigative agencies ending up with more information overall, because they are able to collect information about every encounter with a suspect from law enforcement at the border or participating state and local jurisdictions.

The first step to establishing an organized crime watch-listing system is to create a central repository for the information, along the lines of the Terrorist Screening Center that manages the Terrorist Screening Database. There is currently no central place for information to be shared among the federal, state, and local law enforcement agencies with an interest in countering organized crime, let alone with international counterparts. The applications for this kind of information would be enormous, from vetting law enforcement job applicants to identifying international travelers who should be subject to greater scrutiny to determining whether shipments of goods are coming from companies with connections to criminal organizations. Some of the entities within the U.S. government already have partial repositories of the necessary information:

- The DEA's Special Operations Group consolidates information from investigative databases, but focuses on drug trafficking and responds to queries about specific cases rather than the kind of analysis that would support intelligence-driven law enforcement operations.
- The Organized Crime Drug Enforcement Task Force (OCDETF, referred to as oh-sid-deft) Fusion Center* combines investigative files but only in support of investigations, which in effect means only in support of the Department of Justice law enforcement components and, occasionally, ICE.
- The El Paso Intelligence Center (EPIC) was established by the DEA in 1972 to create a single center where all of the relevant law enforcement agencies involved in countering Southwest border narcotics trafficking could send representatives to facilitate information requests back to their home agencies. Sadly, it has not made a great deal of progress since, and the different representatives must still ask each agency for access to another agency's data.

---

* A fusion center is basically any location where representatives from different law enforcement agencies work together with the express purpose of improving information sharing. There are dozens of these around the country and they range from a few people sitting in a room without access to each other's systems to locations where all of the information is pooled and can be searched at once.

Despite repeated efforts, the DHS relationship with EPIC is particularly fraught.

- The National Targeting Center, which is operated by CBP and vets all international travelers, has an enormous amount of information about travel and interactions with individuals, but does not contain investigative data. If there is a watch list hit the officers must contact the investigative agency to find out more about the threat that has been identified.
- DHS has also established fusion centers around the country to enable coordination with state and local law enforcement, but these tend to provide one-off assistance rather than integrated systems to share information.

The recently created National Vetting Center, which is housed within CBP, could provide the central clearinghouse for this information. This would be a significant departure from its publicly announced purpose, which is to vet refugee applicants and migrants, but an organized crime information clearinghouse would provide a much greater benefit and avoid duplicating the already extensive counterterrorism vetting systems.

Emergency Medical Response

As the types of disasters evolve and increase in scale and complexity, FEMA and the U.S. government are increasingly being tested by challenges that exceed the capabilities of traditional disaster management structures. One major systemic issue that has caused recent difficulties is how disasters that fall outside of FEMA's purview are managed, especially events where the responsible agency is Health and Human Services, such as pandemic disease response. The problems with federal emergency medical response were demonstrated in the discussion of Ebola response in the introduction, where the domestic response was far more disorganized than the international assistance led by CDC and the military.

Federal public health agencies are not organized for emergency response, and the resources are nearly all at the state or local level. One of FEMA's strengths is setting up cross-departmental emergency response involving key state, local, and other stakeholders. Disasters with a major public health component currently lie between the authorities of several different entities, and make setting up this kind of organization difficult.

Health and Human Services is not well positioned to coordinate in this way, and the CDC and the National Institutes of Health have traditionally focused on research and actually fought against reallocating funding for preparedness.[21] As a result, DHS is not effectively positioned to lead the response to emergencies like pandemics, but Health and Human Services is also unable to effectively fill this role. State and local authorities do not spend their time doing strategic planning for national crisis response, and as a result protocols and plans will continue to have be developed as emergencies occur. This also means that processes to distribute vaccines and medicine in emergencies would largely need to be developed as situations develop, which would be particularly concerning in the kind of panicked environment that would follow an attack using a biological weapon.

It is also extremely important to effectively communicate with the public when a disaster occurs. Doctors and technical experts may be correct on the facts but wrong in the approaches that they recommend because they do not adequately factor in the importance of communicating clearly with the public and preventing the kind of public hysteria that can overwhelm officials in the midst of an event.

As a result, the response to these kind of disasters ends up being managed through the White House–coordinated national security policy process at the deputy secretary level, or by the appointment of a special official. In one example, in the wake of the unaccompanied children crisis in 2014 FEMA established a unified coordination group, but because of difficulties in coordination between FEMA and HHS the response was essentially run through the White House's Deputies Committee meetings. The response to Zika was largely managed by the office of the deputy homeland security advisor, also in the NSC. This kind of approach is not sustainable, and new structures and capabilities are going to have to be put into place in order to ensure that the government is prepared to deal with situations like biological threats and handle the rapid expansion of hospital capacity along with the large-scale distribution of medical countermeasures.

Coronavirus Reponse

I wrote the description of the problems with emergency medical response above before the coronavirus had emerged in China in 2019. The loss of life is already staggering as this text is being finalized in early April 2020, and all indications are that the weeks and months ahead will be simply horrifying.

The disorganization and incompetence of the Trump administration's response to the crisis has been well documented, and I am sure the coming months will reveal stunning stories of ineptitude. Two and a half months since the first case of coronavirus in the United States, it still isn't clear who is in charge of the response. The U.S. government does not have a clear pre-established structure for disease response, so it is essential that a single lead be quickly designated and put in a position of authority. In the case of Ebola, President Obama quickly saw that the existing structure was inadequate and that a whole-of-government response needed to be directed by a senior official with real stature from within the White House.

The problem is not just that Donald Trump is a very bad manager, however, or that his son-in-law is worse. Just as it was in response to a migration crisis, the Trump administration's response to disease is fundamentally a twentieth century, nation-state approach. Even if they had been managerially competent, they would not have seen coronavirus as the national security threat that it is. They couldn't understand a pandemic disease as a serious threat until the catastrophe had already started.

This is shown by the security priorities they pursued in the first three years of the administration. They disbanded the directorate in the NSC that deals with pandemic response, because to them it wasn't real national security. National security is supporting regime change in Venezuela and using weapons sales as chess pieces in the Middle East. This is also why the last few years have seen record military budgets while the CDC's budget and medical stockpiles were repeatedly slashed. DHS spent the last three years almost solely focused on stopping migration across the Southwest border and building an irrelevant wall, with little or no bandwidth for other public safety responsibilities.

The inadequacy of a nation-state security approach is also shown clearly by the administration's main priority once the disease arrived in America: a ban on travel from China. The idea that travel restrictions, which were partial at best, would be sufficient to stop the spread of this disease after it had already been found in the United States was just baffling. Meanwhile testing, ensuring supplies of medical equipment, expanding hospital capacity, and other concrete steps that could have been taken to address serious vulnerabilities were all neglected. The awful outcome of this has made it abundantly clear that keeping civilians safe from threats that don't come from foreign militaries will require finding and addressing domestic vulnerabilities.

Conclusion

National security is no longer something that happens in other countries. American civilians and their interests are increasingly vulnerable to threats from nonstate actors. Nonstate actors are also changing and getting more dangerous, in response to societal changes that emphasize individual opportunity. Terrorist organizations especially are changing to become more deadly, which is exceptionally concerning given the technological advances that will enable proliferating weapons of mass destruction.

The government of the United States has begun to respond to these changes after the 9/11 attacks, but is still beginning a process that will take years and be extremely difficult. The most significant step to date has been the establishment of DHS, which consolidated border management and is otherwise an awkward fit for its stated purpose of preventing another 9/11-like attack. The Trump administration's nationalist strategy and managerial disfunction have set this process back and made it more likely that changes will be made after crises occur.

Homeland security problems need a different analytical framework than the military or foreign policy problems with which Americans are familiar. DHS also needs to be understood as it is actually structured and actually functions.

The changes in passenger vetting and targeting have been extensive and are an example of the kinds of shifts that are going to have to occur in other areas to match the changing strategic environment. Twenty-first-century travel security uses extensive information sharing, continuously updated watch lists, rigorous verification of identities, advanced technology, and extensive industry partnerships to secure the flows of travel without major economic consequences.

Migration and border security remain extremely challenging. The border security enterprise that the United States has constructed is mismatched with the types of migrants who are now arriving. Effectively managing migration in a market-state context will require different criteria than have been used in the past and a major expansion of humanitarian admissions.

There are three areas in particular where market-state challenges are straining the organization of the government. Cybersecurity is the highest profile transnational threat, yet the U.S. government is only effectively structured to respond to attributable actions from foreign countries or prosecutable crimes by identifiable actors. Market-state organized crime is extremely dangerous and requires the kind of active disruption that is now applied to terrorist groups, but the orientation of American law enforcement is still to investigate, arrest, extradite, and prosecute. Emergency medical response needs to be made a top priority of federal health officials, and effective structures have to be put into place to respond to the increasing impacts of disease and the possibility of biological weapons.

The strategies and structures that have served us well in the past will now fail to protect us. Adapting to this fundamental change will be extremely difficult, but Americans managed a similar process reasonably successfully in the Cold War. It will take constant engagement and vigilance to prevent the kinds of abuses and overreach that will constantly tempt anxious officials and to honestly identify and address vulnerabilities before disasters occur, in particular by directly and comprehensively confronting the proliferation of weapons of mass destruction. Most important throughout all of this will be a habit of not dodging things because we are afraid of them. The devastation caused by the coronavirus pandemic has clearly demonstrated how unprepared the U.S. government is and how vulnerable Americans have become.

Acknowledgments

I owe too much to too many former colleagues and friends to describe adequately here, so I will thank the people who directly supported this book and particularly those who were generous enough to actually read the various drafts I went through.

I have been profoundly lucky in the friends I've made throughout my life, and several of them are now my business partners. I've now worked with Alan Bersin on too many projects to count, and he has been a remarkable mentor and friend since he first sent me off to learn about ports of entry in 2009. His frank feedback on several early drafts improved the book enormously. Nate Bruggeman is the smartest colleague and the best complement for me that I've ever worked with. He read early versions and, even more importantly, was subjected to and improved my developing ideas in our regular long conversations. Nate always grasps the bigger picture faster than I do. Dave Hansell is the best possible person with whom to do awesome stuff that might or might not work involving drones, radiation, and cargo containers in a Houston parking lot, and has been extremely supportive and patient as I've disappeared for stretches to work on this book.

Chap Lawson has been constantly encouraging and gracious since I first worked for him in the most remote corner of the Reagan Building's fourth floor, and gave me extensive, excellent comments on multiple versions and a great deal of help understanding academic publishing.

Heath Druzin has been a close friend since an elementary school soccer coach let us name our team (we chose "The Bloody Bad Boys"), and was invaluable as a reader from outside of the DHS world. He was patient and encouraging and gently helped me understand just how boring some of my initial draft was. He is in no way responsible for boring parts that remain.

A sincere thanks to the University of Michigan Press for their support for a book about homeland security policy, and particularly to Elizabeth

Demers for being a great advocate and being so patient with all of my questions.

Steph is simply the best and most important person in my life. Charlie will be very happy to know that the book is no longer stuck in Dada's computer. And Josie will no doubt be glad that we can move on to some different topics for our discussions throughout the day.

Notes

CHAPTER 1

1. Governor's councils are discussed in Janet Napolitano, *How Safe Are We? Homeland Security since 9/11* (PublicAffairs, 2019), 14; civil defense is discussed in Juliette Kayyem, *Security Mom* (Simon and Schuster, 2016), 38.

2. "September 11 Terror Attacks Fast Facts," CNN, https://www.cnn.com/2013/07/27/us/september-11-anniversary-fast-facts/index.html accessed 9/17/19

3. "Hurricane Katrina Statistics Fast Facts," CNN, https://www.cnn.com/2013/08/23/us/hurricane-katrina-statistics-fast-facts/index.html accessed 9/17/19

4. Michael D. Intriligator and Abdullah Toukan, "Terrorism and Weapons of Mass Destruction," in *Countering Terrorism and WMD*, ed. Peter Katona, John P. Sullivan, and Michael D. Intriligator (Routledge, 2006).

5. Stewart Baker, *Skating on Stilts: Why We Aren't Stopping Tomorrow's Terrorism* (Hoover Institution Press, 2010), 13.

6. Background can be found here http://www.iata.org/pressroom/pr/Pages/2016-10-18-02.aspx and here http://www.iata.org/about/Pages/history-growth-and-development.aspx

7. U.S Department of Commerce, *United States Summary: 2010. Population and Housing Unit Counts*, September 2012, https://www.census.gov/prod/cen2010/cph-2-1.pdf

8. Michael Chertoff, *Homeland Security: Assessing the First Five Years* (University of Pennsylvania Press, 2009), 11.

9. Molly Billings, "The Influenza Panic of 1918," Stanford University, 1997, https://virus.stanford.edu/uda/

10. "Antimicrobial Resistance Fact Sheet," *World Health Organization*, January 2018, http://www.who.int/mediacentre/factsheets/fs194/en/

11. Internet World Stats, https://www.internetworldstats.com/emarketing.htm

12. James Somers, "The Coming Software Apocalypse," *Atlantic*, September 26, 2017, https://www.theatlantic.com/technology/archive/2017/09/saving-the-world-from-code/540393/

13. Somers, "Coming Software Apocalypse."

14. Clive Irving and Joseph Cox, "Could Terrorists Hack an Airplane? The Government Just Did," *Daily Beast*, November 17, 2017, https://www.thedailybeast.com/could-terrorists-hack-an-airplane-the-government-just-did

15. McKinsey and Company, "Global Flows in a Digital Age: How Trade, Finance, and People Connect the World Economy," https://www.mckinsey.de/files/140425_globalflows_full.pdf page 23

16. Mark Levinson, *The Box* (Princeton University Press, 2006), 80.

17. Rose George, *90 Percent of Everything: Inside Shipping, the Invisible Industry That Puts Clothes on Your Back, Gas in Your Car, and Food on Your Plate* (Metropolitan Books, 2013).

18. "The Geography of Transport Systems," https://transportgeography.org/?page_id=4125

19. Bryan Burrough, *Public Enemies: America's Greatest Crime Wave and the Birth of the FBI, 1933–34* (Penguin Books, 2004), 16.

20. Baker, *Skating on Stilts*, 14 and 15.

21. Baker, *Skating on Stilts*, 163.

22. Pam Bensen, "Panetta: Cyber Threat Is Pre-p/11 Moment," *CNN*, October 12, 2012, http://security.blogs.cnn.com/2012/10/12/panetta-cyber-threat-is-pre-911-moment/

23. Levi Maxey, "Homeland Security Council Urges Action before 'Cyber 9/11' Strikes," *The Cipher Brief*, August 27, 2017, https://www.thecipherbrief.com/home land-security-council-urges-action-cyber-911-strikes

24. A description of the program can be found at http://www.atlanticcouncil.org/programs/brent-scowcroft-center/cyber-statecraft/cyber-9–12

25. Mark Thompson, "Iranian Cyber Attack on New York Dam Shows the Future of War," *Time Magazine*, March 24, 2016, http://time.com/4270728/iran-cyber-attack-dam-fbi/

26. Philip Bobbitt, *The Shield of Achilles: War, Peace, and the Course of History* (Anchor Books, 2002), 229.

27. Philip Bobbitt, *Terror and Consent: The Wars for the Twenty-First Century* (Anchor Books, 2008), 9.

28. Bobbitt, *Terror and Consent*, 46–62.

29. Taken from http://www.independent.co.uk/news/uk/ira-city-bombers-iden tified-by-police-1533278.html, http://news.bbc.co.uk/onthisday/hi/dates/stories/april/24/newsid 2523000/2523345.stm, and http://news.bbc.co.uk/onthisday/hi/dates/stories/february/10/newsid_2539000/2539265.stm

30. "The Nuclear Bomb of Islam," referenced in Nuclear Terrorism Fact Sheet, https://www.belfercenter.org/publication/nuclear-terrorism-fact-sheet

31. Liz Sly, "The Hidden Hand behind the Islamic State Militants? Saddam Hussein's," *Washington Post*, April 4, 2015, https://www.washingtonpost.com/world/middle_east/the-hidden-hand-behind-the-islamic-state-militants-saddam-husse ins/2015/04/04/aa97676c-cc32–11e4-8730-4f473416e759_story.html?utm_term=.15c44d1250b4

32. Lawrence Wright, *The Looming Tower: Al-Qaeda and the Road to 9/11* (Vintage, 2006).

33. Richard Clarke, *Against all Enemies* (Free Press, 2004), the 9/11 Commission Report.

34. Richard Danzig, Marc Sageman, Terrance Leighton, Lloyd Hough, Hidemi Yuki, Rui Kotani and Zachary M. Hosford, "Aum Shinrikyo: Insights into How Ter-

rorists Develop Biological and Chemical Weapons," *Center for a New American Security*, July 2011, 5, http://files.cnas.org.s3.amazonaws.com/documents/CNAS_AumShinrikyo_Danzig_1.pdf

35. Graham Allison, *Nuclear Terrorism: The Ultimate Preventable Catastrophe* (Owl Books, 2004), 41, 42.

36. "Countering Violent Extremism: Actions Needed to Define Strategy and Assess Progress of Federal Efforts," Government Accountability Office, April 2017, https://www.gao.gov/assets/690/683984.pdf

37. Morgan Winsor, "Alleged New Zealand Mosque Shooter Pleads Not Guilty," *ABC News*, June 14, 2019, https://abcnews.go.com/International/alleged-zealand-mosque-shooter-pleads-guilty/story?id=63708704

38. Jessica Stark Rivinius, "Proportion of Terrorist Attacks by Religious and Right-Wing Extremists on the Rise in the U.S.," National Consortium for the Study of Terrorism and Responses to Terrorism, November 2, 2017, http://www.start.umd.edu/news/proportion-terrorist-attacks-religious-and-right-wing-extremists-rise-united-states

39. "Anti-Government Militia Groups Grew by More Than One-Third in the Last Year," Southern Poverty Law Center, January 4, 2016, https://www.splcenter.org/news/2016/01/04/antigovernment-militia-groups-grew-more-one-third-last-year

40. Peter Maas, *Underboss: Sammy the Bull Gravano's Story of Life in the Mafia* (HarperCollins, 1997), 130–31.

41. Maas, *Underboss*, 114–15.

42. Ioan Grillo, *El Narco: Inside Mexico's Criminal Insurgency* (Bloomsbury Press, 2011), 43.

43. Grillo, *El Narco*, 105–6.

44. Evan Osnos, *Age of Ambition: Chasing Fortune, Truth, and Faith in the New China* (Farrar, Straus and Giroux, 2014), 252.

45. Masha Gessen, *The Man without a Face: The Unlikely Rise of Vladimir Putin* (Riverhead Books, 2012), 254.

46. "All 107 Aboard Killed as Colombian Jet Explodes," *New York Times*, November 28, 1989, http://www.nytimes.com/1989/11/28/world/all-107-aboard-killed-as-colombian-jet-explodes.html

47. "52 Killed in Attack on Mexican Casino," *CNN*, August 26, 2011, http://www.cnn.com/2011/WORLD/americas/08/26/mexico.attack/index.html

48. Qiao Liang and Wang Xiangsui, *Unrestricted Warfare* (PLA Literature and Arts Publishing House, 1999), 41.

49. Qiao and Wang, *Unrestricted Warfare*, 26, 29.

50. Qiao and Wang, *Unrestricted Warfare*, 56.

51. Michelle Nichols, "North Korea Shipments to Syria Chemical Arms Agency Intercepted: UN Report," Reuters, August 21, 2017, https://www.reuters.com/article/us-northkorea-syria-un/north-korea-shipments-to-syria-chemical-arms-agency-intercepted-u-n-report-idUSKCN1B12G2

52. William Langewiesche, "The Wrath of Khan," *Atlantic*, November 2005, https://www.theatlantic.com/magazine/archive/2005/11/the-wrath-of-khan/304333/

53. Kim Zetter, "An Unprecedented Look at Stuxnet, the World's First Digital Weapon," *Wired*, November 3, 2014, https://www.wired.com/2014/11/countdown-to-zero-day-stuxnet/

54. "Iran Nuclear Deal: Key Details," *BBC*, October 13, 2017, http://www.bbc.com/news/world-middle-east-33521655

55. "Iran Nuclear Deal."

56. Allison, *Nuclear Terrorism*, 87.

57. Allison, *Nuclear Terrorism*, 10.

58. Allison, *Nuclear Terrorism*, 222.

59. Allison, *Nuclear Terrorism*, 9–10.

60. Rolf Mowatt-Larssen, "Al Qaeda's Pursuit of Weapons of Mass Destruction: The Authoritative Timeline," *Foreign Policy*, January 25, 2010, https://foreignpolicy.com/2010/01/25/al-qaedas-pursuit-of-weapons-of-mass-destruction/

61. Allison, *Nuclear Terrorism*, 20.

62. Allison, *Nuclear Terrorism*, 26.

63. Allison, *Nuclear Terrorism*, 31.

64. Baker, *Skating on Stilts*, 22, 23.

65. Baker, *Skating on Stilts*, 277.

66. Kai Kupferschmidt, "A Paper Showing How to Make a Smallpox Cousin Just Got Published: Critics Wonder Why," *Science*, January 19, 2018, http://www.sciencemag.org/news/2018/01/paper-showing-how-make-smallpox-cousin-just-got-published-critics-wonder-why

67. See https://www.nytimes.com/2017/12/28/climate/trump-tweet-global-warming.html and https://www.cnn.com/2015/02/26/politics/james-inhofe-snow-ball-climate-change/index.html

68. Geoffrey Parker, *Global Crisis: War, Climate Change, and Catastrophe in the Seventeenth Century* (Yale University Press, 2014), xxxii.

69. National Oceanic and Atmospheric Association, LuAnn Dahlman, "Climate Change: Global Temperature," September 11, 2017, https://www.climate.gov/news-features/understanding-climate/climate-change-global-temperature

70. Parker, *Global Crisis*, 16.

71. "Explaining Extreme Events from a Climate Perspective," *Bulletin of the American Meteorological Society*, https://www.ametsoc.org/ams/index.cfm/publications/bulletin-of-the-american-meteorological-society-bams/explaining-extreme-events-from-a-climate-perspective/

72. United Nations Framework Convention on Climate Change, http://newsroom.unfccc.int/nature-s-role/wmo-report-the-escalating-impacts-of-climate-related-natural-disasters/

CHAPTER 2

1. Janet Napolitano, *How Safe Are We? Homeland Security since 9/11* (Public Affairs, 2019), 15.

2. For background, https://www.un.org/disarmament/wmd/bio/

3. Stewart Baker, *Skating on Stilts: Why We Aren't Stopping Tomorrow's Terrorism* (Hoover Institution Press, 2010), 325.

4. "Your Apps Know Where You Were Last Night, and They're Not Keeping It Secret," *New York Times*, December 10, 2018, https://www.nytimes.com/interactive/2018/12/10/business/location-data-privacy-apps.html

5. See *United States vs. Martinez-Fuerte*, 1973, http://caselaw.findlaw.com/us-supreme-court/428/543.html

6. Baker, *Skating on Stilts*, 100.

7. Directive published on April 27, 2016, https://ec.europa.eu/home-affairs/what-we-do/policies/police-cooperation/information-exchange/pnr_en

8. Alex Samuels, "Texas Lt. Gov. Dan Patrick and NRA Feud over Background Checks," *Texas Tribune*, September 6, 2019, https://www.texastribune.org/2019/09/06/texas-dan-patrick-nra-feud-gun-background-checks/

9. Anya Kamenetz, "To Prevent School Shootings, Districts Are Surveilling Kids' Online Lives," *National Public Radio*, September 12, 2019, https://www.npr.org/2019/09/12/752341188/when-school-safety-becomes-school-surveillance

10. Napolitano, *How Safe Are We?*, 78.

11. Jennifer Valentino-DeVries, "Hundreds of Apps Can Empower Stalkers to Track Their Victims," *New York Times,* May 19, 2018, https://www.nytimes.com/2018/05/19/technology/phone-apps-stalking.html

12. Taken from www.cbp.gov statistics and summaries, see https://www.cbp.gov/newsroom/stats/sw-border-migration and https://www.cbp.gov/sites/default/files/assets/documents/2019-Mar/bp-southwest-border-sector-apps-fy1960-fy2018.pdf

13. Camilo Montoya-Galvez, "Military to Spend a Month Painting Border Barriers to 'Improve Aesthetic Appearance,'" *CBS News*, June 7, 2019, https://www.cbsnews.com/news/military-to-spend-a-month-painting-border-barriers-to-improve-aesthetic-appearance/

14. Jerry Markon and David Nakamura, "U.S. Plans Raids to Deport Families Who Surged across the Border," *Washington Post*, December 23, 2015, https://www.washingtonpost.com/politics/us-plans-raids-to-deport-families-who-surged-across-border/2015/12/23/034fc954-a9bd-11e5-8058-480b572b4aae_story.html?utm_term=.b42b4986262a

CHAPTER 3

1. From https://www.dhs.gov/dhs-budget and https://comptroller.defense.gov/Budget-Materials/

2. For the text of the act, see https://www.cia.gov/library/readingroom/docs/1947-07-26.pdf

3. For NSA Directive 1, see https://www.nsa.gov/Portals/70/documents/news-features/declassified-documents/nsa-60th-timeline/1950s/19530101_1950_Doc_3978795_NSADirective1.pdf

4. This story is told in Bryan Burrough's *Public Enemies: America's Greatest Crime Wave and the Birth of the FBI, 1933–34* (Penguin Books, 2005).

5. Available here, https://history.defense.gov/Portals/70/Documents/dod_reforms/Goldwater-NicholsDoDReordAct1986.pdf

6. Max Holland, "The Assassination Tapes," *Atlantic*, June 2004, https://www.theatlantic.com/magazine/archive/2004/06/the-assassination-tapes/302964/

7. Ewan MacAskill, "The CIA Has a Long History of Helping to Kill Leaders around the World," *Guardian*, May 2017, https://www.theguardian.com/us-news/2017/may/05/cia-long-history-kill-leaders-around-the-world-north-korea

8. Background on the Church Committee is available on the senate.gov site: https://www.senate.gov/artandhistory/history/common/investigations/Church Committee.htm

9. David Halberstam, *The Best and the Brightest* (Random House, 1969), 145–49.

10. Tom Ridge, *The Test of Our Times: America under Siege . . . And How We Can Be Safe Again* (St. Martin's, 2009), 127.

11. Ridge, *Test of Our Times*, 130.

12. Juliette Kayyem, *Security Mom* (Simon and Schuster, 2016), 88–89.

13. Stewart Baker, *Skating on Stilts: Why We Aren't Stopping Tomorrow's Terrorism* (Hoover Institution Press, 2010), 168.

14. Ridge, *Test of Our Times*, 162.

15. Dan De Luce and Mosheh Gains, "Pentagon Is Last Holdout as Stephen Miller Tries to Slash the Number of Refugees Allowed in US," *NBC News*, September 20, 2019, https://www.nbcnews.com/politics/immigration/pentagon-last-holdout-stephen-miller-tries-slash-number-refugees-allowed-n1056526

16. Fred Kaplan, *Dark Territory: The Secret History of Cyber War* (Simon and Schuster, 2016), 151.

CHAPTER 4

1. Jerry Markon, "DHS Tackles Endless Morale Problems with Seemingly Endless Studies," *Washington Post*, February 20, 2015, https://www.washingtonpost.com/politics/homeland-security-has-done-little-for-low-morale-but-study-it—repeatedly/2015/02/20/f626eba8-b15c-11e4—886b-c22184f27c35_story.html

2. Brian Bennett, "Red Team Uses Disguises, Ingenuity to Expose TSA Vulnerabilities," *Los Angeles Times*, June 2, 2015, https://www.latimes.com/nation/nation-now/la-na-tsa-screeners-20150602-story.html

3. Janet Napolitano, *How Safe Are We? Homeland Security since 9/11* (Public Affairs, 2019), 9.

4. Chris Perez, "US Has More Spanish Speakers Than Spain," *New York Post*, June 29, 2015, https://nypost.com/2015/06/29/us-has-more-spanish-speakers-than-spain/

5. The president's 2018 budget ended up requesting only $1.6 billion for the wall; see https://www.dhs.gov/sites/default/files/publications/DHS%20FY18%20BIB%20Final.pdf

6. The executive order was subsequently revised twice and the third version was

upheld by the Supreme Court; see https://www.lawfareblog.com/supreme-court-travel-ban-ruling-summary

CHAPTER 5

1. Background from uscis.gov, https://www.uscis.gov/history-and-genealogy/our-history/commissioners-and-directors
2. "John Hancock," History.com, https://www.history.com/topics/american-revolution/john-hancock
3. Anne Quito, "One Historic Meeting Determined the Size and Shape of Every Passport in the World Today," *Quartz*, October 28, 2017, https://qz.com/1111001/passport-design-worldwide-was-first-standardized-by-the-league-of-nations-paris-conference-of-1920/
4. Alan Riding, *Distant Neighbors: A Portrait of the Mexicans* (Vintage Books, 1989), 45.
5. Riding, *Distant Neighbors*.
6. Peter Hopkirk, *The Great Game* (Kodansha America, 1994).
7. Olivier Razac, *Barbed Wire: A Political History* (New Press, 2002), 5–37.
8. Agency background taken from cbp.gov, https://www.cbp.gov/border-secu rity/along-us-borders/history
9. Agency background taken from uscis.gov, https://www.uscis.gov/history-and-genealogy/our-history/agency-history/era-restriction
10. *United States of America v. Ahmed Ressam*, https://web.archive.org/web/20120301162643/http://nefafoundation.org/miscellaneous/FeaturedDocs/U.S._v_Ressam_Complaint.pdf
11. Stewart Baker, *Skating on Stilts: Why We Aren't Stopping Tomorrow's Terrorism* (Stanford: Hoover Institution Press, 2010), 31–37.
12. Baker, *Skating on Stilts*, 60.
13. Baker, *Skating on Stilts*, 64.
14. Baker, *Skating on Stilts*, 67–68.

CHAPTER 6

1. Michael Elliot, "The Shoe Bomber's World," *Time Magazine*, February 16, 2002, http://content.time.com/time/world/article/0,8599,203478,00.html
2. "Agent Infiltrated Terror Cell, U.S. Says," *CNN*, August 11, 2006, http://www.cnn.com/2006/US/08/10/us.security/index.html
3. David Ariosto and Deborah Feyerick, "Christmas Day Bomber Sentenced to Life in Prison," *CNN*, February 17, 2012, https://www.cnn.com/2012/02/16/justice/michigan-underwear-bomber-sentencing/index.html
4. Lorraine Adams with Ayesha Nasir, "Inside the Mind of the Times Square Bomber," *Guardian*, September 18, 2010, https://www.theguardian.com/world/2010/sep/19/times-square-bomber

5. Jon Leyne, "Printer Cartridge Plot Planning Revealed," *BBC*, November 22, 2010, http://www.bbc.com/news/world-middle-east-11812874

6. All of the background on TIDE and the TSDB in this section were taken from the publicly available information on the National Counter Terrorism Center's website, including https://www.nctc.gov/docs/tide_fact_sheet.pdf

7. Description of TECS is taken from the publicly available privacy impact assessment done by Homeland Security in 2011, https://www.Homeland Security.gov/xlibrary/assets/privacy/privacy-pia-cbp-tecs-sar-update.pdf

8. Department of Homeland Security, Office of Biometric Identity Management Identification Services, https://www.Homeland Security.gov/obim-biometric-identification-services

9. Stephen Flynn, *America the Vulnerable: How Our Government Is Failing to Protect Us from Terrorism* (HarperCollins, 2004), 87.

10. Congressional Budget Office, "Scanning and Imaging Shipping Containers Overseas: Costs and Alternatives," https://www.cbo.gov/sites/default/files/114th-congress-2015-2016/reports/51478-Shipping-Containers-OneCol.pdf

11. Congressional Budget Office, "Scanning and Imaging Shipping Containers Overseas."

12. Rose George, *90 Percent of Everything: Inside Shipping, the Invisible Industry That Puts Clothes on Your Back, Gas in Your Car, and Food on Your Plate* (Metropolitan Books, 2013), 10.

13. George, *90 Percent of Everything*, 82.

14. George, *90 Percent of Everything*, 9.

15. George, *90 Percent of Everything*, 22.

16. George, *90 Percent of Everything*, 69 and 107.

17. George, *90 Percent of Everything*, 40.

18. Flynn, *America the Vulnerable*, 109.

19. George, *90 Percent of Everything*, 41.

20. Graham Allison, *Nuclear Terrorism: The Ultimate Preventable Catastrophe* (Owl Books, 2004), 105.

21. George, *90 Percent of Everything*, 41; and Allison, *Nuclear Terrorism*, 110.

22. Allison, *Nuclear Terrorism*, 61.

23. George, *90 Percent of Everything*, 43.

CHAPTER 7

1. Ha-Joon Chan, *23 Things They Don't Teach You about Capitalism* (Bloomsbury Press, 2010).

2. Monte Reel, "Underworld: How the Sinaloa Drug Cartel Digs Its Tunnels," *New Yorker*, August 3, 2015, https://www.newyorker.com/magazine/2015/08/03/underworld-monte-reel

3. All totals are taken from https://www.cbp.gov/sites/default/files/assets/documents/2019-Mar/bp-southwest-border-sector-apps-fy1960-fy2018.pdf

4. Statistics are updated at https://www.ice.gov/detention-management

5. Mexican enforcement numbers taken from https://www.npr.

org/2019/07/13/740009105/how-mexico-beefs-up-immigration-enforcement-to-meet-trumps-terms

6. Statistics taken from https://www.cbp.gov/newsroom/stats/sw-border-migration

7. "Coolidge Signs Immigration Act of 1924," History.com, https://www.history.com/this-day-in-history/coolidge-signs-stringent-immigration-law

8. "Senate Passes Immigration Bill," *Politico*, June 28, 2013, https://www.politico.com/story/2013/06/immigration-bill-2013-senate-passes-093530

9. Janet Napolitano, *How Safe Are We? Homeland Security since 9/11* (Public Affairs, 2019), 59.

CHAPTER 8

1. Fred Kaplan, *Dark Territory: The Secret History of Cyber War* (Simon and Schuster, 2016), 48.

2. Charles McCarry, *The Better Angels* (E. P. Dutton, 1979).

3. Patricia Zengerle and Megan Cassella, "Millions More Americans Hit by Government Personnel Data Attacks," Reuters, July 9, 2015, https://www.reuters.com/article/us-cybersecurity-usa/millions-more-americans-hit-by-government-personnel-data-hack-idUSKCN0PJ2M420150709

4. "Equifax Data Breach Affected 2.4 Million More Consumers: Total Now at 148 Million," *Consumer Reports*, March 1, 2018, https://www.consumerreports.org/credit-bureaus/equifax-data-breach-was-bigger-than-previously-reported/

5. Information is available at https://support.apple.com/en-us/HT208108

6. Ben Popper, "Amazon Key Is a New Service That Lets Couriers Unlock Your Front Door," *The Verge*, October 25, 2017, https://www.theverge.com/2017/10/25/16538834/amazon-key-in-home-delivery-unlock-door-prime-cloud-cam-smart-lock

7. Maggie Astor, "Your Roomba May Be Mapping Your Home, Collecting Data That Could Be Shared," *New York Times*, July 25, 2017, https://www.nytimes.com/2017/07/25/technology/roomba-irobot-data-privacy.html

8. Superior Court of the State of California, "Declaration of Samuel Ward Spangenberg Filed in Opposition to Defendant's Motion to Compel Arbitration," October 5, 2016, https://www.documentcloud.org/documents/3227535-Spangenberg-Declaration.html

9. Ethan Wolff-Mann, "Gmail 'Smart Reply' Feature Is a Reminder Google Scans Your Email," *Yahoo Finance*, June 2, 2017, https://finance.yahoo.com/news/gmail-smart-reply-feature-reminder-google-scans-email-200758158.html

10. John Lanchester, "You Are the Product," *London Review of Books*, August 17, 2017, https://www.lrb.co.uk/v39/n16/john-lanchester/you-are-the-product

11. See https://obamawhitehouse.archives.gov/the-press-office/2016/07/26/presidential-policy-directive-united-states-cyber-incident

12. Stewart Baker, *Skating on Stilts: Why We Aren't Stopping Tomorrow's Terrorism* (Hoover Institution Press, 2010), 228.

13. Lee Ferrin, "Here Is the Indictment against Russians Accused of Election

Intrusion," *ABC News*, March 24, 2019, https://abcnews.go.com/Politics/indict ment-russian-election-intrusion/story?id=61147180

14. Kaplan, *Dark Territory*, 185.

15. Kaplan, *Dark Territory*, 34.

16. Kaplan, *Dark Territory*, 138.

17. Kaplan, *Dark Territory*, 178–79.

18. Kaplan, *Dark Territory*, 280–82.

19. "Promoting Private Sector Cybersecurity Information Sharing," https:// obamawhitehouse.archives.gov/the-press-office/2015/02/13/executive-order-pro moting-private-sector-cybersecurity-information-shari

20. Janet Napolitano, *How Safe Are We? Homeland Security since 9/11* (Public Affairs, 2019), 160.

21. Tom Ridge, *The Test of Our Times: America under Siege . . . and How We Can Be Safe Again* (St. Martin's, 2009), 114.

Index

166 | Index

Cold War nuclear threat, 11
Colonialism, driving national boundaries, 90–91
Comprehensive Immigration Reform, 131–34
Computer Security Act of 1987, 142
Congress, 7, 8, 47, 68, 69
    horse trading when DHS was created, 48
    oversight of DHS 68–69
Container security, 114–17
Container Security Initiative, 116
Containerization, 16–17
Coronavirus, ix, 12, 149–50
Counterterrorism, 49, 51
COVID-19, ix, 149–50
Cross-border tunnels, 124
Customs and Border Protection (CBP), 38, 39, 57, 58, 77–81, 104, 105, 108, 109, 112, 113
    Centers of Excellence and Expertise, 112
    formation of CBP, 49
    use of facial recognition, 105–7
Customs racketeering, 88
Customs Service (legacy customs later absorbed into Customs and Border Protection), 49, 50, 88
Customs-Trade Partnership Against Terrorism (C-TPAT), 111
Cyber 9/11, 18, 137, 138
Cyber Command, 142, 143
Cyber Pearl Harbor, 137
Cybersecurity, 15, 16, 18, 19, 137–43
    and Iranian government dam hack in New York state, 19
Cybersecurity and Infrastructure Security Agency (CISA), 63, 64

Dean, Diana, 94
Department of Defense, 8, 13, 45, 46, 52–54
    Cold War failures, 13, 46
    Goldwater-Nichols reforms 13, 46
    military bases used in response to flows of unaccompanied children, 53

Posse Comitatus Act, 53–54
    resistance to domestic responsibilities, 52–54
    role in homeland security 52–54
Department of Justice, 43, 48, 50, 51, 127
Department of Homeland Security (DHS)
    entities that joined DHS, 47
    formation of DHS, 47–48
    international role, 69, 70
    management and challenges, 63–66
    mission, 55
    morale, 64, 65
    organization and operational components, 56–63
    oversight, 68, 69
    participation in NSC meetings, 64
    role in North America, 70–72
    role responding to infectious disease 4–5
    working with State and Justice, 70
Development, Relief, and Education for Alien Minors (DREAM act), 120, 121
Domestic Policy Council, 52
Drug Enforcement Administration, 144–47
Drug resistant diseases, 15
Drug smuggling, 123, 124
Duncan, Thomas Eric, 1–4

Ebola, 1–5, 52
Einstein 2 project, 143
El Paso Intelligence Center, 147
Electronic System for Travel Authorization (ESTA), 98, 102
Emergency medical response, 1–5, 148, 149
Entry/Exit, 106, 107
Equifax, 140
Erika (fuel tanker), 114
Executive Office for Immigration Review (Justice), 127

Facebook, 141
Federal Bureau of Investigation (FBI), 18, 46, 48–51, 95, 143, 144

Made in the USA
Monee, IL
24 January 2022

89712736R00105